T0207947

in love with bangladesh

The Heart of a Missionary

JILL HANSON FLATT

WestBow
PRESS
A DIVISION OF THOMAS NELSON

Scriptures taken from the Holy Bible, New International Version®, NIV®. Copyright © 1973, 1978, 1984, 2011 by Biblica, Inc.™ Used by permission of Zondervan. All rights reserved worldwide. www.zondervan.com The "NIV" and "New International Version" are trademarks registered in the United States Patent and Trademark Office by Biblica, Inc.™

Scripture quotations taken from the New American Standard Bible®, Copyright © 1960, 1962, 1963, 1968, 1971, 1972, 1973, 1975, 1977, 1995 by The Lockman Foundation. Used by permission." (www.Lockman.org)

Edited by Jeannie Lockerbie Stephenson
Cover by Ken Underwood

WestBow Press books may be ordered through booksellers or by contacting:

WestBow Press
A Division of Thomas Nelson
1663 Liberty Drive
Bloomington, IN 47403
www.westbowpress.com
1 (866) 928-1240

ISBN: 978-1-4908-1948-8 (sc)
ISBN: 978-1-4908-1949-5 (hc)
ISBN: 978-1-4908-1947-1 (e)

Library of Congress Control Number: 2013922445

Printed in the United States of America.

WestBow Press rev. date: 01/13/2014

Contents

* signifies that a term can be found in the appendices. Many cultural and medical terms are detailed in the appendices.

About the Cover

The image on the cover of this book is taken from a piece of original artwork by Surayia Rahman called a *nakshi kantha*. Nakshi kantha, a specific embroidery work, is the national handicraft of Bangladesh. Often nakshis are done using threads from old saris. More intricate designs can be accomplished with silk on silk materials. Each piece represents weeks to months of labor from one of the hard working ladies.

The piece featured on the cover is from the first project started by Friends of Bangladesh. The Widows Sewing Center is located in a large slum north of Dhaka. After the 1971 Bangladesh Liberation War, many women were left alone and unable to support themselves. The sewing center is full of laughter and joy, expressions of happiness not always seen in the slum. There, two hundred women are fed and educated in a Christ-centered environment while they sit together making delicate, intricate embroidery pieces.

The nakshis are marketed in the United States for the income generation project. The money from the pieces sold is used to feed, clothe, educate, and care for the ladies who make them. A missionary is on staff at the site to help run the project and reach out to the ladies' tender hearts. Faith Willard, Friends of Bangladesh executive director, carries the pieces back to the United States when she comes a couple of times a year.

The nakshis feature both scenes of Bangladesh life and skillfully, artfully done scriptures. The quality is the best in Bangladesh, and they are breathtakingly beautiful. If you have any interest in hanging one on your wall or supporting the widows who create them, please contact Friends of Bangladesh. Further information about the organization at the back of the book.

To my beautiful kids, Graham and Grace

This book was written for you, because I want you to remember me in a way you never even knew me. My wish for you is to understand the purpose of sacrifice. You two have given me the drive to keep going when I would have rather given up. I love you both and will continue to pray that you will grow into the plans God has laid out for you. Those plans may be scary at times, but I hope they will be dreams come true—as mine has been.

Acknowledgments

Many people deserve thanks for their roles in bringing this book to fruition. Thanks to my husband, Richard, who has loved me through all the tougher times, for richer or for poorer, in sickness and in health. My parents, Hank and Chris Hanson, and sister, Valerie Blair, have had to walk through so much of this journey with me. They have endured what many families never have to. My dear friend, Starla Wright, I give you credit for keeping me alive through some of those tough times back in Bangladesh. Thank you, Nancy Walter, for encouraging me to when I had already given up on this dream by convincing me to write this book as something to pass on to my children. Thank you, all, for always supporting me.

On the technical end, Cindy Scinto helped to spur me on. She had written about her experiences as a heart transplant patient and graciously met with me to discuss how to turn a manuscript into a book. When I was sending out letters to procure permission to use quotes, Jeannie Lockerbie Stephenson offered her assistance in editing. She had been a larger-than-life hero to me for thirty years already, and I never dreamed of having her help in writing a book of my own.

Every person mentioned in this text has played a role in more than just a book. I often say that my favorite gifts from the Lord are the ones He wraps so beautifully in human skin. God has so blessed me with precious people who mean the world to me. Each person mentioned here is so dearly loved.

Thanks most of all to Jesus for giving me a dream and then making it come true.

Introduction

This book is a love story, a love for a nation and a love for God. Bangladesh has meant more to me over the course of my lifetime than any person, place, or thing. When I was introduced to the country in junior high, a relationship began that shaped the rest of my life. Ephesians 2:10 states, "We are His workmanship, created in Christ Jesus for good works which God prepared beforehand so that we should walk in them" (NASB).

I found what God had prepared for me to do, and I went after it with all my being.

This book documents the journey of a love for all things Bengali, tied together with a love for Christ. In spite of dangers and complicated situations, God has given me a relentless love for Bangladesh and His people there. The Lord has led me in and out of Bangladesh several times, each instance under the most dramatic of circumstances. As I shared my stories of these experiences with friends and churches over the years, many suggested that I write about the grand adventures I have known in a lifetime of intimately walking with Christ. Others have told me they have been blessed and challenged by what they have seen the Lord do in my life. My desire to see people draw near to the Lord finally compelled me to commit the words in my heart to paper.

The story increasingly became what I really didn't want it to be at all. I lost all enthusiasm and hope for encouraging others with it. This journey with Christ has amazed even me with so many fantastic experiences, but a few devastating twists as well. I always planned to write this book to inspire people and make them excited to go and share the gospel where the Lord is not yet known. In 1993, an infection in my heart changed my life and my future. The heart problem I acquired through viral myocarditis★ ultimately came to require constant attention. I doubted anyone would feel drawn to go serve the Lord when the cost could be so devastating. I certainly didn't think it to be a very victorious story anymore. I still long for God to continue to use me any way He will so that some may come to know His saving power. Finding ways to serve Him continues to bring me great joy.

Mostly, this book is about a dream come true. God gave me a dream and fulfilled it by moving His mighty hand. I dreamed of Bengalis worshipping at the throne of Christ when all the saints are home in heaven someday. Awesome displays of His majesty presented again and again while I sought to follow Him for all I was worth—wherever He might lead. As I've tried to follow with all my heart, all my soul, and all my mind, the rewards have been staggering.

My mom said so many times, "How is it that you seem to get everything you want?" I had one easy answer for that: "Delight yourself in the Lord, and He will give you the desires of your heart" (Psalm 37:4).

CHAPTER 1

The Desires of My Heart

*Delight yourself in the Lord, and he will
give you the desires of your heart.*
—Psalm 37:4

An angry mob gathered at the Rupsha River crossing point in Khulna, Bangladesh, brandishing knives, clubs, and whatever primitive weapons were at their disposal. Shouts of political protests energized the masses. The mosque had called for blood, and the faithful were responding. This was Bangladesh in the fervor of a political strike. Mine was the only white face in the crowd, and the blood they were out for was mine. *How did I ever come to be in this place and in this situation?*

I don't really remember life before Christ. My family moved from California to Washington State the summer I turned five. I went forward at an altar call all by myself, when I went to my Uncle Mike and Aunt Karen's church. Though I can't profess I fully understand the theological ramifications, I sincerely gave my life to Christ that fall of 1972. I was only five years old, and I asked Jesus into my heart.

1

Occasionally, over the years, I relaxed in the intensity of my walk with Christ. Even that much separation from God, however, was really too sad, too lonely, and a real eye-opener to how desperate a life without Christ must really be. I rededicated my life several times in the first few years of my faith walk, just to be sure.

I earned my first Bible at vacation Bible school at the age of six. Luckily, I was a good reader, because it was the King James Version. I did the best I could with it. My mother regularly took me to church, but I read my Bible and prayed with no real input from my parents. I always sensed a heartfelt connection with Him to whom I had given my life. I still have that Bible with the inscription from the VBS speaker, a ventriloquist and his puppet, that reads, "Johnny and I will be praying for you."

Fast forward to when I was about twelve years old. I was tiny, shy, smart, and a conservative evangelical—almost all to an extreme. Everything was neat and tidy: my world, my room, my homework, my nature/environmentalist club. Friends would ask if I could come over and play, but I was generally too busy reading books and listening to radio preachers. I knew them all via KMBI (the local Moody Bible Institute station) and listened from right after school until two o'clock in the morning. I had terrible insomnia, so I used the time when I couldn't sleep for reading and praying until Bill Pearce came on the air with his *Night Sounds* program—which I'm sure I never heard all the way through.

A watershed event occurred when I was in junior high, a routine thing that unexpectedly changed my life forever. My social studies teacher, Mr. Ketcham, gave our class an assignment to write reports on various countries. When the time came for everyone to choose a country, I was at home, sick with tonsillitis. By the time I returned to school, most of the known world was taken. I had vaguely heard of Bangladesh, so I chose that country.

I approached the assignment with my usual style, reading everything I could find and even interviewing a missionary who was home from Bangladesh. The book *Daktar: Diplomat in Bangladesh*, by Dr. Viggo B. Olsen and Jeanette Lockerbie, really opened my eyes and heart. Even to this day, I know more about the history of the Indian subcontinent than I do about America.

What I really took away from that school report was that Bangladesh was a hurting country in desperate need of prayer. I purposefully hung a map on the wall in my bedroom. At that young age, I committed myself to pray every day for the people of the feeble little new nation of Bangladesh. More than thirty years later, I don't think I have missed a day.

In high school, I slowly grew to be less small and less shy but remained very nerdy smart and all the more evangelical. All my best friends, including my boyfriend, came to know the Lord kneeling at the side of my bunk bed.

Corrie ten Boom (author of *The Hiding Place* and famous for hiding Jews during WWII) is quoted, "We never know how God will answer our prayers, but we can expect that He will get us involved in His plan for the answer. If we are true intercessors, we must be ready to take part in God's work on behalf of the people for whom we pray."[1] My commitment to Bangladesh gradually took on a new form as well. I felt the Lord telling me prayer was not all I could offer. I began to feel that Bangladesh missions would be part of my future and started praying and preparing to that end.

My parents, who had both made commitments to the Lord by this point, thought that I was a strange kid with a strange preoccupation that would eventually pass. At that point, they did not recognize it as a desire in my heart planted by years of abiding in Christ.

Not all was perfect in my world. Some things came tumbling apart when I was seventeen. The chaos and unpredictability of life became unmanageable. Unknowingly and unwittingly, I had created my own little inner world where I was my own God. That summer, as I lost control of my kingdom, I learned important spiritual lessons. Broken by a series of disappointments, the death of a close friend, and the shattered images of people I held in high esteem, I tried to take my own life. When that too failed, I was bitter and sarcastic and caustic in my discussions with Jesus. *Okay, Mr. All-Things-Work-Together-for-Good, what can you do with this mess?*

Once again, Jesus did not fail me. I have been able to use those dark experiences to help guide other people in their own spiritual journeys. All our experiences shape us into who we are, so I have learned to be thankful for even those dark times.

In 1985, I graduated from Mead High School in Spokane, Washington, and left home for Seattle Pacific University (SPU), a great Christian university. There I prepared academically and spiritually for missionary nursing. A vision had formed of a ministry of feeding the hungry, healing the sick, and telling people of the coming kingdom of God. Since I am not able to say, "Rise up and walk," I imagined starting a medical clinic someday in the land of my dreams: Bangladesh.

Thoughts of mobile clinics and of sharing Christ with Muslim women motivated me. I majored in nursing and minored in cross-cultural ministries. Once, the SPU dean of nursing had a meeting with me to "discuss my priorities." She could not grasp that my dream was not to be *just* a nurse. Rather, nursing was a tool to be used in sharing Christ in Bangladesh. Academic advisors, in both the School of Nursing and the School of Religion, were confident that they had the more significant role to contribute.

God spoke Psalm 37:4 to my heart repeatedly. "Delight yourself in the Lord, and He will give you the desires of your heart" resonated, often as a challenge, to find my delight in Him. As the verse promised, when I obeyed, the rest naturally followed.

The first time we had a guest speaker for our SPU nursing program was the beginning of God's unfolding of a dream before me. We were sophomores, just starting in the actual nursing school. Our speaker—Rebecca (Becky) Davey, an SPU alumni—said, "Before I tell you anything about who I am or what I do, let me show you a little video." She pushed in the videotape and up came the title, *Daktar: Story of a Mission Hospital.*

Nobody in that class was more captivated than me. My eyes welled with tears, which started to roll down my cheeks. She was *the* head nurse from *the* hospital from *the* book that had initially inspired me. I was excited to think how God might use me someday.

A few years later, Becky was SPU's "Alum of the Year." She inspires me still. I consider her a mentor. At the time, her coming was proof positive for me that SPU would prepare me well for a future in Bangladesh. I love the fact that now I have been granted the same opportunity to speak to and inspire young nurses as well. May some find themselves in Bangladesh someday.

Bangladesh was my obvious choice when it was academic report time at SPU. During the research process, I got to meet my first Bengali, Albert. He was studying in Seattle while living with retired missionaries just blocks from Seattle Pacific. Meeting him encouraged me as I eagerly prepared myself in every way I could to serve God in the country He had laid so firmly on my heart.

My years at SPU were a busy time of ministry and growing deeper in my walk with the Lord. I was involved in Bible studies, street ministry, and prison ministry. My knowledge from my two years of high school Spanish was stretched as I did evangelism among the Hispanic urban Seattle subculture. I attended *El Templo del Reyador* (a Pentecostal Hispanic church) in West Seattle so I would have a church to take the street people to. I took four or five people each Sunday evening for about a year and discipled several of them both on Sundays and several other nights through the week at the Sonshine Inn Coffee House. The Inn was a ministry of the Union Gospel Mission for the homeless people on the streets of Seattle.

My Spanish improved, and I was soon leading Bible studies in Spanish at the prison in Shelton, Washington, one Sunday each month. I never worried about my safety in the prison or on the streets, because I always felt securely tucked under God's wing. I felt completely in the will of God and was confident that I was safe. I had so many friends who were prisoners and street people that I really was about the safest person on the streets of Seattle. In two years of going out on the streets, late into the nights for three or four nights each week, I never got a scratch or a bruise. I was never even threatened.

My sophomore year I was the Urban Involvement (UI) coordinator, facilitating and organizing urban ministries for the whole university. I was also a student ministry coordinator (SMC) that year, leading Bible studies for the girls on my floor at Ashton Hall. Life was full of ministry and activity in addition to a full-time, heavy academic class schedule.

For a while, it was too full. Busy with classes, work, orchestra, ministry, and friends, sleep was the first thing to go. I resented every minute of sleep my body demanded. I eventually became sick, developed ulcers, and nearly suffered a nervous breakdown. During that overwhelming time, in a two-week period during the fall quarter, five people I knew died in five different incidents. First, one of our beloved SPU professors had a heart attack and didn't survive. One of the street people I worked with was knifed to death. My dear Uncle Tom, my mom's brother, was killed in a motorcycle accident. An elementary school friend died of cancer. Then my childhood neighbor, by that time a very old man, died a peaceful death. It was all a bit much for a nineteen-year-old to process. I quit answering the phone for fear of someone telling me of another person who had died.

Consequently, during that time I experienced a grueling six weeks without sleeping. I went to my classes, work, and all the many activities, but I was a walking shell. I didn't get anything done, not even homework. When I got myself together, I talked to my professors who had noticed the "university scholar" honor student not doing any assignments. I was told if I could get the papers in by the end of the semester, they wouldn't be marked late. So I did a paper a night until the school break and went home to sleep for the whole Christmas holiday. I ended up in counseling briefly, but really just looking at what Jesus endured for me helped me to regain my perspective. Probably the sleep, and being away from assignments for a while, helped too.

> Some wish to live within the sound of a chapel bell, but I want to run a rescue shop within a yard of Hell.
> —C. T. Studd[2]

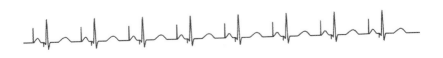

CHAPTER 2

My First Trip, 1988

i thank christ jesus our lord, who has
given me strength, that he considered
me faithful, appointing me to his service.
—I timothy 1:12

In my junior year at SPU, I was able to get recentered again—
academically, personally, and spiritually. The Lord began to
bring together the many pieces He had used in preparing me
over the years.

SPU had a short-term missions program called SPRINT
(Seattle Pacific Reach-out INTernational). Because of the time
commitment and financial issues, I thought it would be something
my parents would not agree to. In fact, I never even looked into
the SPRINT program. I was already prepared for spending an
academic summer in Costa Rica in the summer holistic nursing
quarter. The SPRINT application deadline came and went
without my paying any attention at all.

One SPRINT team was being co-led by some friends of
mine from my missions classes, Steve Young and Kathy Teigen.
After the deadline had passed, Kathy and Steve were still asking

me to apply for this special SPRINT team. Normally, I saw them about only once a week in our classes, but for the next few days they bumped into me everywhere. They just kept asking me, praying, and urging me to pray. Along with praying, I did some investigation.

The trip was to be an experiment of sorts. The people on the team seemed to be handpicked, though I didn't know that at the time. All six members of the team had traveled cross-culturally before. All six of us spoke more than one language, and all were either missions majors or minors at SPU. The purpose was to study mission strategies, spending a month each in Thailand, India, and Pakistan. The university missiology professor, Dr. Thomas Wisley, was coming for the first month.

India is very close to Bangladesh geographically; that fact did not escape me, and I could imagine the possibilities. Though the deadline had passed, I applied and was immediately accepted. When I turned in the remaining paperwork, however, a major stall ensued. The Student Ministry Office decided because of my gastric ulcers and mononucleosis that semester, they couldn't let me go. How could that be? I hadn't planned on going initially, but now I really wanted to be a part of the team.

I went to my doctor and asked him to repeat the upper GI series and liver function tests. Not surprisingly to me, the numbers and pictures were back within normal limits. That is what I like to call seeing God "flex" His mighty arm. It was not even reasonable to expect a different result, but I knew the Lord had a plan—and He wasn't going to let little a lab work interfere.

That hurdle was cleared, but I wasn't sure how to approach my parents on the subject. In a calculated move, I excitedly told them I had an opportunity to go to Lebanon for the summer, in the midst of a war. (I had already spent one scary summer in a war zone, in Northern Ireland, when I was sixteen. I had traveled with my Oma to where she had immigrated from, visiting her family with her where I was very impacted by seeing the violence of the conflict in Ireland up close.) My dad was near tears wondering why I wanted to go to such awful places. When I confessed that I actually had a chance to go to Bangladesh, they acknowledged that at least they had been given some time to adjust to that idea over the years. I had been praying for Bangladesh for eight years by then. They gave their consent.

As part of my multifaceted preparation, I went to the mosque in Seattle one day. I had arranged an interview but went to listen and observe first. Not expecting to understand anything really, I just went to see how the service proceeded.

This was the first of a few experiences I would have with the Lord as my translator. I thoroughly expected the Lord to be my guide, but not necessarily my interpreter. I followed the service in its entirety, though it was in Arabic. I understood it in a way that allowed me to ask pointed questions in the interview and to share my love of Christ at that special meeting. As we read in Job 37:5, "He does great things beyond our understanding." It was an extraordinary moment to share with the Lord. What a thrill to share experiences with the Lord that displayed His power so obviously.

At that time, preparing to travel in South Asia required many immunizations. On one trip to the King County Public Health Department, I received three shots, including a typhoid★ vaccine in one arm and a cholera★ shot in the other. The next morning, I was surprised to find that I had huge red welts on each arm and was unable to lift my arms at all. My college roommate, Kimmy Clark, had to help me get dressed.

Kimmy later had to endure the uncertainty of proximity when I was diagnosed with a mild case of the plague—the black plague.* Because I was planning to go into rural Bangladesh, I had decided to get all the shots, whether mandatory or just mildly recommended. The vaccine series elicited a mild case of the plague during my obstetric rotation of nursing school. The infection control department of the hospital had to clear my even being allowed into the building. It felt as if I had leprosy, although I was in a place where no more leprosy existed. (It does still exist in Bangladesh however.)

Some good-byes were necessary before leaving. Though I was only going away for the summer, it seemed an incomprehensibly long time to the three-year-old boy for whom I frequently babysat. I watched Zachary often, because he had busy parents. Zachary had a tough time accepting the idea that I would not be around all summer. When I picked him up at preschool for the last time, he presented a gift to me so I wouldn't forget him. He scrunched his cute, chunky hand into his front pocket and pulled out five little pebbles that he had thoughtfully collected. I gushed over how great they were and thanked him profusely, promising to keep them close.

That same weekend—the Sunday before we left—at Bethany Community Church in Seattle, Pastor John McCullough preached a poignant sermon on David and his five smooth stones. I carried those five little rocks with me for many years, all through Asia. They were a tangible reminder to me both of a special love with a precious little boy and even more so of a promise given to me. Though I was not strong enough on my own to conquer the giants I would be facing, I knew the Lord was on my side and victory was eminent.

So began the trial team: SPRINT Asia. We were to go the farthest distance ever, to the poorest places, in more than one country, for the longest SPRINT outreach ever. It was an outreach SPU never repeated.

The trip was planned for three months instead of the usual three weeks. We had some successes and learned plenty in that time; however, in other ways, major failures occurred. We barely eluded being the first SPRINT team to have everyone hospitalized. Among the six of us, we lost over one hundred fifty pounds. We were all sickly and skinny when we returned, despite all the shots we had taken to prevent illnesses.

Dr. Thomas Wisley, SPU missiology professor and former missionary to Thailand, came with us for the first month. He conveyed strategies to reach the Buddhist world for Christ, translated for us, and worked to ready us for the next couple of months when he would not be with us. We prepared dramas and songs to present to the people we encountered. In fact, we had been preparing for months prior by fund-raising, undergoing academic preparation, and—most importantly—preparing spiritually.

We took turns with our parts in the presentations. At Payap University in Chiang Mai, Thailand, it was my turn to present the gospel narration to go along with our drama of the "Broken Heart." For me, this was another extraordinary moment from the Lord. I sought the Lord in the morning, asking Him to clearly speak His words through me. I felt His power and His presence as He answered in an unexpected way. Though a translator stood beside me on the podium as I spoke, she interpreted nothing at all, standing speechless beside me. However, five hundred kids sat absolutely captivated by words that shouldn't have made any sense. To this day, I have no idea how they were understood at all. Either those Thai students were able to understand my English as a gift from the Lord, or maybe they even understood the message in Thai with God Himself as the translator. They connected with me as if I were speaking Thai. Maybe I was.

When the drama was over, I was completely unable, like before, to transcend the language barrier. God showed up in a mighty way that day for us to experience. He would not have our shortcomings stand in the way of His message. The young people responded to the words of the Lord and all were blessed, including us. The response, of both the interpreters and the team, was a quiet, respectful awe—an acknowledgment of seeing God's power displayed.

I had really wanted to learn about third-world medicine on the trip. It just so happened that I got my chance. In Bangkok, Stacey was hospitalized with typhoid. Doug was hospitalized with stomach problems in Northern Thailand. We all ended up with terrible food poisoning early in our trip, after we had lunch on the floor in a pig barn at the farm project we were working on in Udon Thani, Thailand.

In Kolkata, India, a spell of alarming, frequent diarrhea about turned me inside out. I initially didn't recognize how severe the dehydration was, even while I was lying on the bathroom floor in my own vomit and stool. I hadn't urinated for a couple of days because I was so dehydrated. I was admitted to "the best hospital in Kolkata"; yet as a patient caught in a cholera epidemic, I was admitted to the OB ward. My roommate was a woman who was sixteen days post-op gallbladder surgery and smelled like death. It was a nightmare but definitely a learning experience.

Even in that horror, we saw God at work. I met a terrified British woman who was married to an Indian. She was having her first baby and felt reassured by having six Western Christians nearby. The Lord drew close to her at the hospital through us.

The hospital bed mattress was made from coconut fibers (with all kinds of biological fluids in them). Since there were no glass panes in the windows, I shared the bathroom—where I spent most of my time—with crows and lizards. Upon admission to the hospital, a nurse approached me with what looked to be a rusty needle to offer me medication to stop throwing up. I declined. I had no idea if the next needle for the IV fluids was clean or not, but I knew I needed it regardless. The nurse set the intravenous fluids to drip in slowly. When she left me, I unclamped the tubing to pour in the much-needed fluids. The poor nurse came back in panic-stricken to slow it down, and I had to wait for my next chance to increase the flow.

I learned about third-world medicine in a way I hadn't expected. When it was over, I was thankful for the experience. But before that, I actually tried to escape. I attempted to leave in the middle of the night, against medical advice, after feeling well enough to get out of bed. That rather harrowing episode was unsuccessful in the end. After making to the back seat of a taxi with Kathy, the driver asked if I was a patient. Though I told him "not anymore," he couldn't leave with all the people surrounding the car. I ended up sitting on the bed for the rest of the night until Doug came and straightened things out and got me officially discharged.

Back at Lee Memorial Guest House in Kolkata, after my stay in the hospital, I pondered how I had picked up cholera. As I sat weary and weak on the porch, watching the constant buzz of Kolkata sprawl, the community well across the street provided the answer to that question in vivid *National Geographic* detail. I watched as some people drew water to cook, others bathed, and others brushed their teeth and spit. It was no wonder cholera spread so easily. The diarrhea is so profound that many Indians die within twelve hours of onset.

14

Before I left for this trip, my greatest apprehension was not about being sick but about what my response would be to seeing people dying on the streets. The book *The City of Joy*, by Domique LaPierre, accurately details the city in many ways. I felt as if I both knew the people and could get around the city just from having read the book.

I had studied about destitute people living in the streets of Kolkata and its enormous surrounding slums. This was nothing like the street population I had worked with back in Seattle. One Sunday morning, we were walking to church and there he was—a middle-aged man (probably actually quite young) lay in the final stages of dying right before our eyes. I felt as if the parable of the good Samaritan was playing out before my eyes. *What am I supposed to do?* I had no place to take him, and we were expected to speak at a church in a few minutes time. So we followed our guide and continued on our way. On the way home, we saw his dead body. The crows had already descended upon him. Ugh, I still hate crows.

On another walking outing, I reached the point of just crying and trembling uncontrollably as I looked out at Kolkata. The clanging, the honking, the noises made me jump, and every beggar I passed by made me physically shudder. The pleas of so many maimed, blind, leprous, and desperately poverty-stricken people were overwhelming as they reached out their dirty empty hands. Their eyes would pierce my heart. Big booms sounding like cannon fire could be heard occasionally from the transformers blowing from the massive draw on the power infrastructure. We had to get into a taxi to go the rest of the way for fear that I would collapse into a sobbing heap on the streets. The six of us spent the summer taking care of each other as needed in ways just like this.

This was a learning experience for us all. Later I came to know Kolkata better and knew whom to call and how to deal with these situations, but it was a crushing experience in the beginning. I came to help, but I found some things to be far beyond what I could manage.

I learned valuable practical and spiritual lessons from volunteering with the Missionaries of Charity ministries in the city. As Mother Teresa said, we served Christ in the "distressing disguise of the poor." We visited leprasariums, the Shishu Bhavan★ orphanage, and the famous house of dying destitutes: Nirmal Hriday. The sisters at Kalighat, as it is otherwise known, were informed that I was studying nursing and proceeded to present problems and ask for my input. The boils and abscesses, like I had only seen in books, haunt me still. Though they implored me to intervene, I lacked the confidence and experience to do much. In later years, I determined that I really did have more information to share. I taught the sisters how to treat bedsores, which were devastatingly prevalent in the starving, dying population they served.

We also served with Arunoday Rehabilitation Centre for drug addicts, which was run by Vijayan Pabamani, an expert on drug rehabilitation in India. He also ran an amazing ministry where street kids were gathered off Howrah Train Station platform and grew to love the Lord while they were raised as Christians to become future leaders of India.

Kolkata was overwhelming from entry onward. Our contacts picked us up at Dum Dum airport and told us it was going to be quite a drive into the city because the horn was broken. *Huh?* That made no sense to us at all until we were on the roads. Traffic moves in a terrifying, abstract way. People say the traffic flows like a river, with no clear lanes among the various vehicles on the road.

That ride from the airport was my first exposure to roads full of cars, buses, and trucks mixed with cows, bikes, rickshaws,★

pushcarts, and so much humanity. The streets were lined with people living in unspeakable poverty. The din, the smells, the heavy acrid air assaulted the senses in every way. The city brimmed with fear and spiritual darkness. Idols and altars could be seen every few feet in every direction. These were the outward symbols of people trying to appease the myriad gods of Hinduism in the city of Kali, the goddess of destruction. Yet, while in Kolkata, I experienced one of the most anointed moments of my life up to that point.

As a Christian connected to Bengal, I am a huge admirer of the pioneer missionary William Carey, the translator of the Bengali Bible and father of modern Protestant missions. One of Carey's famous quotes helped motivate me through many challenges: "Expect great things from God; attempt great things for God." In later years while working with Bengali Christians, I learned stories of William Carey that rivaled the Paul Bunyan tall tales I'd heard from my father during my childhood. The descendants of Carey's ministry tell of his work in ways far eclipsing what I had heard in mission history classes. In Khulna, the Christian community talked of his translating Bible pieces containing forty languages singlehandedly—and much more.

What an inspiration to see his name in giant bold letters we walked toward Carey Baptist Church. We sang *And Can It Be* and did our Broken Heart drama piece. Then Pastor Llyod Rainey clipped the microphone onto my shirt. Before me was a congregation of Bengali faces here to worship the Lord—the first Bengali Christians I had actually seen. I felt a surge in my spirit. God had very specifically given me these people to love. His power and His peace washed over me as I felt an affirmation in my soul that I was created to be a missionary to the Bengali people. I was delighting in the Lord, and He was certainly giving to me the desires of my heart. The thrill really came from being appointed to His service. It was a joy to bask in the love of the Lord with His Bengali people that He was so graciously sharing with me.

As this was a Christian community, they could appreciate that someone had it on her heart to go and share Christ with the Muslims across the border in Bangladesh (formerly the state of East Bengal in India before the 1947 partition). With the bloody partition lines drawn, the Bengali speakers of the world had a bold boundary separating the Hindus from the Muslims.

After a month in India, the team moved on as planned to Pakistan. While in Pakistan, we stayed at a SERVE missionary guesthouse in Peshawar, near the Khyber Pass to Afghanistan. The missionaries from the SERVE house took us everywhere and were our guides, teachers, and translators. One of the SPRINT team guys would jokingly tease us girls if we didn't jump to do what he asked. He would yell "Two camels, two camels" as if to sell us on the spot. Women were treated as commodities in Pakistan, and many willing buyers were available. I struggled more than I had expected to with the culture.

A plane was shot down on August 17, 1988, shortly after our arrival in Pakistan. This caused a great deal of trouble for Americans in Pakistan at the time. Many heads of state—including the ruling dictator General Zia-ul-Haq, the US ambassador, and two dozen senior military officers—were killed in that crash. We were contacted by the American Embassy and told to stay indoors and out of sight. For ten days, we received daily warnings from the Embassy.

Peshawar is a lawless "Wild West" type of town in the East. Men carry bandoliers, and women are rarely seen. I watched one woman in a full burka,★ wondering how she could see at all. While that thought crossed my mind, she stepped into the hem of her garment and fell completely flat on her face. I also have a photo of a newborn Afghan baby lying in a swinging bed made from an ammunition case. We were just miles from the famed Khyber Pass, where the mujahideen crossed into Afghanistan every night to fight. Each night we could hear the explosions across the border. We kept the praying saints at home on their knees to be sure.

The highlight of my time in Pakistan was meeting and spending time with Trudy Winkleman, a lifelong missionary in Central and South Asia. A fellow nurse, she gathered me under her wing and mentored me as to what my role could be as a long-term missionary. Later during my years in Bangladesh, she remained one of my greatest encouragers. She translated for me in the Afghan refugee camps and asked questions of me as if I had something valuable to offer. I remember her listing some symptoms and asking, "Do you think this might be postpartum malaria?"★

One thing that affected me long after this mission ended was a sign at an NGO (nongovernment organization) office from the UNHCR (United Nations High Commission for Refugees). It simply read, "A refugee would love to have your problems." How is that for helping keep perspective?

At church in Peshawar one day, I remember having to sing very quietly so we wouldn't be heard. This was my first time worshipping in a place where a high price could be paid for being discovered as a Christian. The congregation of about twenty people met in a school, behind closed doors. Even without a welcome sign out front or a piano playing, God was among us, as promised in Scripture. I was privileged to meet some secret Christians, and they touched my heart.

After the partition of India in 1947, East Pakistan and West Pakistan were divided by fifteen hundred miles of hostile Hindu territory. In 1971, West Pakistan and East Pakistan fought a bloody civil war for the independence of the new nation of Bangladesh. Pakistan had wronged Bangladesh in so many crucial ways. After the Pakistani army came to Dhaka University campus to kill the educated Bengalis, things could never be brotherly again. Even as Muslim brothers, they could not bridge that gap of distrust and betrayal. After Bangladesh was established as a new nation, no room remained for colonialism.

As a nation, Bangladesh is so new yet that the war is not forgotten at all. In fact, people born before 1947 there were born Indian, became Pakistani with the partition of India, then Bangladeshi citizens after the Liberation War. The Bengalis who were born before the partition had three national identities without ever leaving their village homes.

When I was leaving Pakistan, one missionary lamented, "Well, at least you will still be serving in Pakistan." I realized more and more how biased I am for all things Bangladesh. I felt a sting inside me. They had *won* that war. It was not East Pakistan anymore, and a lot of people had sacrificed their lives to make Bangladesh a reality. I was a supporter of all the freedom fighters, the Mukti Bahini,★ who gave their lives to see the birth of a new nation on the other side of India.

> Even on the low ground of common sense, I seemed to be called to be a missionary. Is the kingdom a harvest field? Then I thought it reasonable that I should seek to work where the work was most abundant and the workers fewest.
> —William Carey

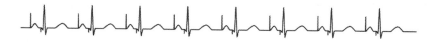

CHAPTER 3

A Dream Come True

leave your country, your family, and
your father's home for a land that i will
show you.
—genesis 12:1 msg

The SPRINT team shared an amazing three months of learning
and serving together. I knew I would miss them after being
so close all summer, but my dream-come-true was just a short
plane ride away. The rest of the SPRINT team escorted me
to Dum Dum airport in Kolkata to say good-bye and see me
off to Chittagong, Bangladesh. Not many people experience a
precise moment when a dream comes true, but mine happened
the afternoon of August 28, 1988. I was glad to be alone, because
this was *my* long anticipated adventure. I changed some Indian
rupees to Bangladeshi *taka*★ before departure. Every moment was
increasingly exciting as Bangladesh became nearer. Only six
passengers flew on the forty-four seat plane for the short flight.
Lunch on the plane was a carrot and green pepper sandwich, a
slice of fruitcake (with a hairball and dirt on top), and an apple
with three wormholes in it. Despite that, I felt a real sense of the

21

Lord being both the maker of my dreams and the one who makes them come true.

I had written to Becky Davey to arrange a visit to Memorial Christian Hospital in Malumghat, Bangladesh. I never heard back from her and had no assurance whatsoever that any of my plans were going to work out. I wondered what I would do if she wasn't there, but I wasn't nervous or worried about it; I was just so thrilled to be actually going to Bangladesh. The flight was breathtaking. I looked out the window transfixed the whole way, in deep conversation with the Lord. In years of imagining, I never pictured how big a delta could really be. Muddy brown water was everywhere, and the land was green like you've never seen green before. I didn't come unglued when we landed, as I feared I might. I just sat motionless on the plane looking out the window, in prayer, completely oblivious to everything around me. When I looked up, everyone else was gone. I remember staring out the window with tears streaming down my face feeling a sense of awe … *this* was *it*.

Two distinct greetings welcomed me to Bangladesh. An Indian man asked as I disembarked, "You're coming as a tourist? Bangladesh isn't a nice place to visit, and I certainly wouldn't want to live here."

The other was more inviting. The stewardess interrupted my solitary moment by saying, "Sister, your Mother is here waiting." Becky Davey, the first missionary speaker at SPU and a nurse mentioned in *Daktar*, had not only received my letter but had come to receive me at the Chittagong airport. I was getting a chance to be tutored by my hero. I stayed with her at the hospital compound for the next week. The sights, sounds, smells, and all that I read of and prayed for were coming to life all around me. Years of dreaming and praying met reality in my world.

My first full day in Bangladesh, I not only got to tour Memorial Christian Hospital at Malumghat, I actually got to lend a hand. Among the missionary staff, a typhoid epidemic raged. A visiting resident MD and I performed two surgical cases that afternoon. He amputated the necrotic leg of a man covered with neurofibromas. He also performed a C-section and hysterectomy on a woman whose baby had died. Her water had broken two months prior. The baby was decomposing, and she was dying of peritonitis. The hospital buzzed with activity and emergencies. A two-day-old baby died.

Another two-month-old baby, weighing only three pounds, was hospitalized for malnutrition.★ Her arms were as small around as my pinky finger. I got to snuggle her as much as I wanted. I spent days in the outpatient department (OPD) seeing case after case of worms,★ scabies,★ malaria, fungal infections, and more. I took notes every day and tried to learn from these people who were so experienced at what I dreamed of doing myself someday.

Becky directed me to a little girl named Halima Khatun. She was from Burma and had been dropped off at the hospital with no family to care for her. It was not known if anyone would be returning for her. I blew up balloons and colored with her to provide some amusement and lighten her day. That was my introduction to the situation in Burma that would end up affecting us in Bangladesh more and more over the years.

It may not have been everyone's idea of the ultimate mission trip, but for me it was what dreams were made of. "Delight yourself in the Lord, and He will give you the desires of your heart" (Psalm 37:4). It is possible to have your dreams come true *if* your dream is that the Lord's will be done in your life. Do not try to put up boundaries on what you want from God. He will not fit in any box; He cannot be contained. Be it riches or the fellowship of the suffering, it will be what is best for you. He will be faithful.

During my seven days on the hospital compound, I often wandered slowly from the house to the hospital across some of the twenty-five acre grounds singing, praying, and marveling that I was actually in Bangladesh. The words of martyred missionary Jim Elliot summed up those days: "Oh, the fullness, pleasure, and sheer excitement of knowing God on earth." I asked questions of everyone I could speak to, and I tried to stay in a receptive cross-cultural mode to absorb as much as I could.

I experienced the joy of going to church at Chabagan, a jungle area that meant "Tea Garden." The Malumghat missionaries worship God alongside Bengali Christians there. The monsoon rains had transformed the path to the church into deep, slippery mud. The walk there with Becky was laughter-filled and laced with adventure for me. We slogged through slippery mud and clay through the jungle in pouring down rain all the way to church ... my face beaming. Both sides of the path were the deep green of rice fields dotted with little mud huts. Church was quite a memorable experience; the sight of a yellow-banded krait, the two-step snake, had many of us standing on the benches.

I love it that no matter where we are, people think of Jesus in their own nationality and as speaking the same language they do. That is especially true of Bengalis, whose national pride is wrapped up in the love of their language. If they were to invite Jesus to dinner, they would serve rice and dhal and curry ... and that would be normal to Him too.

I spent my evenings reading books about Bangladesh, many of them written by missionaries to Bangladesh who were right there at Malumghat. Hearing their stories in person, however, was even more exhilarating. I heard that one of the doctors was asked frequently about the cure for the dreaded consequence of being bitten by a dog. Women were afraid to receive rabies shots, because they feared in their next pregnancy they would deliver puppies.

The longtime missionaries at Memorial Christian Hospital knew a lot about medical missions in Bangladesh and also about the real story of independence for the nation. Some had stayed in the country for the entire war. I often thought one of those missionaries should have been appointed president. In *Daktar*, Dr. Viggo Olsen is granted visa #001 to the newly established independent nation. When I returned to the United States, I had the privilege of carrying the manuscript of *Daktar II* back with me to send to the publisher. I felt so honored to be the courier of such pure gold. A line from the famous, beloved Bengali poet Rabindranath Tagore capture some of the feelings of those days.

> That world lying out there, quietly—I love it
> so much—all the trees, its rivers and the fields,
> the bustle of its thousand people, its solitude, its
> dawns and dusks, how I feel like holding all these
> in my hands.

Another major event happened while I was in Bangladesh that first time. The "biggest flood since Noah" occurred in September 1988. Granted, floods are an annual problem in the monsoon season, but in 1988—between the rain and India's opening the Farakha Barrage—85 percent of the nation was affected by the disaster. Becky told me that Bangladesh gets as much rain in three months as the Olympic rainforest back home in Washington gets in a year.

In the midst of that flood, an unexpected drama also unfolded. Somehow a rumor grew into a report, and I ended up in the news at home—as missing and presumed dead in Bangladesh. The press interviewed my parents. The story was in the papers, on the local news, and on Christian radio stations in Spokane and Seattle. Strangers were calling SPU to blame the university for my death. The scene was set for a strange homecoming.

Malumghat was not actually flooded as badly as the rest of the country. I was to make my return flight on the first plane that flew into the heart of the disaster. Right behind us on the tarmac was the first international relief shipment coming on Aeroflot from the USSR. It didn't look as if I would be able to go to Dhaka. I already had rerouted my flight home to take me out through Kolkata. Those plans changed. I ended up tagging along to join other missionaries for food and blanket distribution. I also went with International Needs as they set up feeding centers. Hundreds of people lined up with empty bowls to get their empty bellies filled. All over the country, on isolated high spots, vast multitudes of people were starving. No place was dry in the rain, and there were only a few places where the water wasn't at least waist deep. We traveled in boats to assist people stranded on the roofs of buildings. Snakes were forced out of their hiding spots, and as many people died from snake bites as from drowning. The infrastructure in Dhaka was insufficient to support the more than ten million people who called it home at that time. The city was a raw sewage wasteland. Some places experienced 100 percent, total decimation—no buildings left standing. Most Muslims (who made up the majority of the population) are not buried in coffins; many dead bodies were unearthed and floated around in the disastrous mess, a human soup of misery.

In spite of the flooding, I was able to visit the orphanage supported by my own Bethany Community Church in Seattle. A young missionary couple named Bob and Twyla McGurty, from the Assemblies of God Church in Dhaka, accompanied us to Savar. They are still treasured friends. Normally a forty-five-minute drive, because of the flooding we had to travel by boat to get to Savar International Needs Children's Village. The journey took over an hour. Along the way, we surveyed the destruction and saw the occasional rooftop poking through the water. All the buildings were damaged. Bob and Twyla showed me a little room on the compound and explained that they hoped it would someday be a clinic. I certainly made a mental note of that (and later sent money regularly to assist with the eventual clinic). As we viewed the devastation, I was struck by the hope of the Christian Bengalis I was with. Even though their homeland was crippled, it was not despair but the unmistakable joy of the Lord that dominated their countenance.

During my time in Dhaka, I had planned on spending a few days in the Bihari★ refugee camp. The plan, so neatly organized in my head, was to leave my belongings at the church and go live "homeless" in their midst to gain a better understanding of the refugee problem. I had studied the Bihari situation for a paper in missiology class at SPU. The Biharis are refugees, Muslims from the state of Bihar in India, who are political remnants from the battle for independence. They have remained stateless all these years. Since they are not Hindus, they do not fit in India well. They also don't belong in Bangladesh, having fought against the Bengalis in the war for independence. I had no idea that my planned visit was an incredibly bad idea. I probably would have been killed right away. Biharis are among the more radical Islamic element in the country. By God's grace, I couldn't go anyway because the whole camp was underwater.

When phone communication were finally restored, I put in a trunk call★ (land line call) to my parents. It can take hours for an operator to be able to get a line for a phone call, as the communication infrastructure in Bangladesh was also insufficient. Dad answered the phone and just started to cry. I was quite puzzled as he passed off the phone saying, "Here, talk to your mother." They didn't tell me then about the local news reports, only that lots of mail awaited me. My mom holds up very well under stress. She later admitted that it wasn't until things were cleared up that she got the worst headache she'd ever had. In that pile of mail, sympathy cards to my parents summed up the horror they must have endured.

Ironically, I knew going into the trip that death was a possibility. I had written letters to those closest to me and put them together in a big envelope marked "to be opened in the event of my death." I gave it to my good college friend Karen, so my parents wouldn't have to know I considered such an eventuality even a remote possibility. I told my sister, Valerie, that if anything happened to me, she was to call Karen. When the news of my so-called "death" was relayed, the reality of what I had asked her to deliver struck Karen. She hesitated, asking if a body had been found, and thankfully my parents heard from me on the phone before they received my letters from the grave. Karen was among those waiting for me at SeaTac airport when I returned home. She let me know, in no uncertain terms, that she wouldn't volunteer for that job again.

I actually returned to Seattle on exactly the day I planned. My plans had been interrupted only during the middle of the journey. All across the SPU campus, people were looking at me like I was a ghost and saying my name like it had a big question mark after it. "Jill?" Mom still hadn't informed me of the news. It turned out to be a great blessing indeed in my eyes. Because so many people cared what happened to *me*, Bangladesh was finally front and center in many people's prayers.

The flood was so devastating that it was leading the world news in September 1988. I had been privileged to experience it myself. The novelty of me having been reported dead led to me being asked to speak at many events. At conferences, church meetings, and even SPU's chapel, I got to lead people in prayer for the lost and struggling, near drowning little country that I love so much. For me, being present for the disaster turned out to be an answer to prayer. In reality, Bangladesh wasn't going to get a whole lot worse than that. I thought if I could be in the midst of that and love it, it should just get easier after that. "Delight yourself in the Lord." Those delights and desires continued to build … to what pointed toward completion of joy. Sharing such a passion with the Lord was a way of sharing in His joy. "That joy is mine, and it is now complete" (John 3:29).

Vacation to the US Center for World Missions

"It's a great to be a Christian caught up in the joy
of God's personal plan! It's great to be a Christian
called to serve in Bangladesh!"

—Dr. Vic Olsen[3]

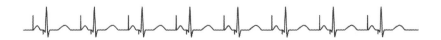

CHAPTER 4

An Unexpected Invitation, 1990

i can do all things through him who strengthens me.
—Philippians 4:13 nasb

God had assured me, to my core, that I was made for Bangladesh. My immediate goal became to finish college and get back to Bangladesh as a career missionary. I started work at Harborview Medical Center when I returned home, first as a student and then as a graduated nurse. Harborview in Seattle had the reputation for being the most challenging hospital to work at. Goal oriented and driven, I reasoned that I had the best chance of learning what I needed most by working at Harborview.

I met Starla Wright at orientation my first day as a new nurse. By the end of the introduction tour, I had seen her heart and knew she was a sister in Christ. We became fast friends. To this day, she remains one of the greatest gifts ever given to me by my God, who knows just what I need. He meets my needs in ways … beyond what I could ask or imagine (Ephesians 3:20).

My work focus was on earning money for Bangladesh and getting the experience I would need to start a clinic there someday. Starla reminded me that I was a rather odd duck. I still lived with Kathy Teigen and Stacey Reynolds from the SPRINT team at the time. They both worked for World Relief refugee resettlement services, and our house was a revolving door of international refugees. A busy schedule of late night trips to SeaTac airport to meet incoming refugees kept that door moving. We had no furniture in the main room—that way we could roll out a bamboo mat and feed as many people as needed to eat. Sometimes strangers slept in the front room as well.

One day, only six months after graduating from college, I got a phone call from Bangladesh. It seemed to come straight from heaven, at least in the sense of "out of the blue." The Bengali director of the orphanage I had visited on my trip called to say they were ready to start the medical clinic at the International Needs Savar Children's Village. Would I like to come and help them get it started? My heart raced and skipped some beats as my dreams were again coming to fruition before my very eyes. International Needs is an NGO that works only with local missionaries. I was being asked to be the only foreign missionary with International Needs in any of the countries where they worked—much to the delight of my Bethany Community Church, who were big supporters of it. Not much persuasion was needed.

As exciting as it was for me to prepare, my parents struggled. My last trip I had been sick and then reported dead. When they declared they really didn't want me to go, I literally ran out the door of my house sobbing to talk to Pastor John at Bethany community church. My Pastor talked to me about my relationship with God and listening to God's call and still honoring my father and mother. As hard as it was for them, it resulted in great spiritual growth for my family as well. Soon they were leading a Bible study and prayer group in our neighborhood. Having me far away and potentially in harm's way taught them to pray at whole new levels.

What a privilege. "Delight yourself in the Lord." My dreams were becoming reality in ways I couldn't have asked or imagined. I know God's Word to be true and that He is able to do exceedingly more than we can fathom. He can blow your mind with the way He will answer prayer when your continued prayer is, "Your will in my life, Lord."

Besides sending money to support the future clinic, I was also sponsoring a couple of orphan children in the Children's Village. I had no remote idea that they would someday ask me to be the one to physically start the clinic in Bangladesh. Mohammed Dulal Miah, one of the young boys I supported, would become another miraculous gift from the hand of God.

The exciting time of preparation was upon me again. Raising money was effortless. People had known my intentions for many years, and many had told me when it was time for me to go I was to send them a support letter. I know it was also easy because God was totally in it. By this time, Starla was my roommate, coworker, and closest friend. She had been hearing nonstop of Bangladesh since the day we met. I was the eccentric missionary-in-training who read biographies all the time, took a vacation to the US Center for World Missions, dressed in Bangladeshi *salwar kameez*★, and ate with my fingers. As I prepared, Starla made it clear that she did not want to be a missionary, but she did want to accompany me to Bangladesh just to see where I would be. It made the whole experience even richer to be sharing it with Starla.

The luggage had a story of its own. I had been packing for months. My whole room was taken over by medical supplies for starting a clinic. The several military footlockers full of medical equipment represented many hours of packing and rearranging. At the airport, however, I learned some of the boxes were far too heavy. Though I had meticulously packed them for weeks, I was forced to take everything out and redistribute them on the spot to try to get each bag under the weight limit. I mixed heavy with light and shuffled quickly and then reweighed the bags. Each bag was within a pound of the allowed limit after just one try.

Starla's first flight ever was over twenty hours long, from Seattle to Bangkok with a stop in Tokyo. After arriving in Bangkok, she and I took a fantastic journey through Thailand and India before going to Bangladesh. We rode a train across Thailand so we could go jungle trekking in the north. We shopped, adventured, and enjoyed the fellowship of our precious friendship. In India, we purchased an Air India pass that allowed us unlimited flights around the country to see the many different areas of the diverse nation. From the Taj Mahal to Gandhi's footsteps, we learned the history of India. From the church in Madras (now Chennai)—where St. Thomas the apostle was said to have first shared Christ—to an accidental participation in a Hindu pilgrimage, we explored the range of the spiritual experience in Hindustan (which was still a nation with more Muslims than most Islamic countries). Starla helped get me started in what would be a very trying period at the Children's Village. After escorting me to Bangladesh, she saw me to the orphanage and then went back to Seattle without me.

I had returned to Bangladesh to use my degree for exactly the purpose I had pursued it, only a year after graduating from nursing school. The plan was to spend the next twelve months at the Children's Village teaching a nursing class and starting the clinic and to reach out to the people of the village. I'd done in-depth research on how to run a clinic and treat tropical diseases.

Before starting out on my journey, I sought out extra training for suturing, casting, and more from physician assistants and nurse practitioners at my church. I memorized nearly the entire book *Where There Is No Doctor*—a must read for third-world clinic medicine and published in nearly every language. The Bangla *QIMP* (Quick Index of Medical Products) was also a daily read, after my Bible. Once in Bangladesh, I visited several established mission clinics learning necessary phrases and procedures. Having been introduced to the clinic at Malumghat first, I then visited as many NGO clinics as I could arrange. The Dhaka International Christian Church (DICC) was a good networking point, as many of the missionaries congregated for church together. I spent a week in a tribal village area in Mymensing, taking notes and drinking in the knowledge of two longtime Bangladesh missionaries from Germany. I studied possible structure and layouts for the organization of a clinic. I determined what equipment was essential and what processes were most effective. As I learned more Bengali, with the help of my tutor, I used it to share the Lord as much as I possibly could.

With 276 children in residence at the International Needs Children's Village, it was nearly impossible to connect closely with them all. I became most familiar with the children who needed to spend the most time in the infirmary. I finally felt like a real missionary, living my ultimate dream. When it was monsoon season and we were flooded into isolation, I set broken bones myself. I delivered babies. I saw twenty to thirty patients per day in the clinic and taught a class in basic nursing skills to a dozen young girls. Each day I was desperate with prayer and exuberant with praise. Ultimately, living with that many non-English speaking orphans was a very effective way to learn the language.

International Needs provided a tutor for me upon arrival. In the early days, my tutor—Mrs. Baroi, who was the English teacher at the Children's Village school—was the only one I could communicate with well. When one of the children, Rebika, needed an abscess drained, Mrs. Baroi had to assist; she was the only one who could take any verbal instructions from me. My hand was so shaky as I went to incise the big abscess that I needed the other hand to steady it. I got a fair start learning Bangla from her, and she provided someone to talk to when I didn't have enough language skills yet to connect.

Monica Didi was also hired to stay with me and look after me. Having househelp is a common practice in Bangladesh. She cooked, cleaned, and followed a step behind me all day, every day to take care of me. Often, she interrupted my seeing clinic patients to be sure I had tea. The administration was in charge of her, and they gave her a spot on my porch where she could sleep. It felt this was too much like putting the dog out for the night. I didn't like that at all, so I had her stay in the room with me. If I would change clothes, she was immediately washing them. At night, she would pull my bed under the fan, put down the mosquito net, and go through the room killing any bugs before telling me that my bed was ready. A couple of times, louder smacking noises resounded as she killed shrews and rats for me.

The clinic room was small, about eight by nine feet, with an attached separate infirmary room containing two cots and an old cabinet. The assortment of medical supplies they had on hand were so ancient I couldn't even recognize them from books. I had brought nursing textbooks and footlockers of supplies. I studied *Where There Is No Doctor* to near memorization and used the Bangla translation to help me learn necessary vocabulary.

The Clinic at International Needs Children's Village

Some dental equipment had been left in the clinic cabinets at Savar by a past visitor. The children all had terrible teeth. With no toothbrushes and paste for them, they didn't even have a fighting chance at it. I got some guidance from another missionary and took up the task of tooth cleaning for them all. The tartar was thick, but the children were patient at letting me spend afternoon playtime cleaning their teeth one day after another. My mom sent toothbrushes that had been donated and collected for them by a dentist in Spokane. When those arrived, the new toothbrushes replaced the fray-tipped neem★ tree twigs for oral care.

Early in my stay, I started worm treatment for all the children to improve their general health. Good nutrition has less positive impact if worms are benefiting from the food. A one-time dose of albendazole is usually effective treatment, a complete cure costing well under a dime. I was just learning Bangla, but I could grasp what the primary topic of discussion centered around for the next few days. The hand motions helped. Everyone was astounded with how many worms they had and how big they were. Worms were so common that I treated all the orphans every six months from that point on. I treated myself too, usually without checking to see if I had worms or not, because really ... who wants to know that? Whenever visitors came, I gave them a parting gift: a dose of albendazole. (I just bought it by the case.)

The biggest task during my stay at the Children's Village was a full scale war on scabies. I could write a whole book just about scabies treatment and its clinical pathways. Scabies is largely considered just a nuisance, but it can be much more serious. There are clinical pathways that can lead ultimately to renal failure and death. It took them seeing the serious repercussions of scabies before I could convince the local leadership to allow me to treat all the children. The first response to my request was that everyone had scabies—it was just a part of living in Bangladesh. The national director and village staff also suggested that these were just orphans in Bangladesh. If everyone else had them, certainly these children would not be exempt. My request to treat them all, using my own money and equipment, was not allowed until after disaster struck.

The Children's Village had two tragic deaths and two more children in renal failure as a result of scabies complications left untreated. A young tribal boy named Ashok was in renal failure, necessitating dialysis at the government hospital. Another boy was being treated with medication for renal failure. The war commenced with 150 children on antibiotics for a week: 100 children taking pills and 50 more getting injections every eight hours. The infirmary had only twenty-five syringes and needles. At my request, Monica Didi focused on equipment six times a day instead of bothering to cook food. I barely ate or slept at all for the entire week. I hand bathed 276 children with soap and scabicidil lotion, heating water myself to bathe them with the rare luxury of warm water. I hauled mattresses to the roof to beat them and expose them to sunlight. The whole Savar Children's Village got involved in the multifaceted battle. A day laborer was hired to cut fifty-five gallon metal drums in half and use them to boil all the clothes and bedding from the whole orphanage compound. It was a long, sleepless week, but the war was won.

I had to leave the country after that week to go get my visa renewed. I went to a beach for a week in Hua Hin, Thailand, and cried from exhaustion. The Juniper Tree, where I stayed, was neither a resort nor a hotel; it was a rest facility only for missionaries working in Asia. Missionaries from around Thailand understood my collapse when they learned I was just out of Bangladesh. I ate, slept, sat on the beach, and read missionary biographies off the shelves of the Juniper Tree as my passport was being processed at the Bangladesh Embassy in Bangkok. On many of my other trips into Thailand I enjoyed the bustle and activity of Bangkok, but after the scabicidal conflict I just needed to recover.

My own *chele*,★ whom I sponsored, became quite ill while I was serving as the nurse at the Children's Village. For a brief period, many of the kids shared a febrile illness. Dulal had one long, brutal seizure-filled week with it. Through his rugged week, I experienced a joy that almost no child sponsor knows. Dulal was delirious with fever and seizures, and then sick from the medicines used to treat them, and finally fatigued from the seizure recovery. He lay on the infirmary bed with his head in my lap while I prayed for my little Muslim boy. I had prayed for him long before I knew I would ever meet him. That connection made him all the more precious. He began to cry out in his sleepy stupor, *"Jishu,* Jishu, Probhu Jishu."* He was calling out to the Lord Jesus.

I wasn't going to hold him accountable for anything he said during that time. When it was over though, and he was fully recovered, he recounted the whole story. *"Ami Jisukhe deckechi"* (I saw Jesus). *"Ami Christian hoichee"* (I became a Christian). He borrowed a cross necklace from another little buddy at the orphanage and never strayed from his claim for the rest of the year. I had held him in my arms while the Lord appeared to him, healed him, and called him His own. It was easy to delight in the Lord.

During the Scabies War, Dulal Pictured on the Left

Living with all those orphans brought unthinkable heartache as well as unspeakable joy. One boy, Robindro, touched my heart in a special way. When I was checking the health of the kids, I found the slight nine-year-old to be quite ill. A lifelong malnutrition had left him blind from the vitamin A deficiency, xerophthalmia.★ When I took him to an optometrist, Robindro could not see the chart at all. The doctor put up fingers in front of Robindro's eyes to ask "how many." The doctor moved closer until his hand was near the end of Robindro's nose. No matter how much Robindro squinted, he could not even see the doctor's hand. Instead of prescribing glasses, the doctor only gave me Robindro's hand and said, "Help this boy." Robindro was also profoundly fatigued, and his heart was failing from long-term protein energy malnutrition. He was dying. I took him out of school so he could rest and enjoy whatever was left of his young life. He considered himself my assistant in the clinic. I built a lot of snacks and naps into the duties of my assistant. By the next year, Robindro had passed away.

Though I occasionally utilized the local medical resources, many times it was better to just manage on my own. One day, a boy named Chitten was playing rough with some of the other kids, as the young boys at the orphanage often did. They brought me the tiny six-year-old after he had been smacked soundly on the head with a stick. He lost consciousness almost immediately. This seemed to be the time to get further help. It took a little time, but we found a driver and vehicle to take him to the local hospital, a short drive away in the town of Savar. A couple of hours later, while Chitten was still unconscious, a nurse attempted to put medicine in his mouth for the headache they assumed he had. I stopped her from giving the unconscious boy anything—a major choking risk—and quickly realized it

41

had been a mistake to take him to the hospital. By the grace of God, he awoke shortly after coming back to Savar—with nothing worse than a headache.

During the monsoon rains, eight-year-old Susama tumbled down the concrete stairs at the orphanage. Her arm was deformed and obviously fractured, but the roads were washed out, making it impossible to get to the hospital. I reduced the fracture with traction and set it with rulers. I secured the rulers with some scarves from the girls' clothing supply and gave her medication for pain. When we were finally able to get out of the village, visiting the X-ray shop was a high priority. The X-ray showed the fracture was well set and healing already. That helped bolster my confidence to manage the care without having to go for help.

Although OB was not my specialty, when one of the International Needs staff was ready for her own delivery, she wanted me to deliver the baby. I agreed, as it was not her first baby and she was a healthy-sized Bengali lady. I was blessed to be involved, but she did all the work really. If I had felt we needed to get extra help, the roads were clear and the car was available. We managed together for a great confidence-building and memory-making experience for us both.

Most of the children's care was managed within the compound walls with me regularly seeking more experienced missionaries for advice. Bina was a defeated little girl. At only seven years old, she had no fight left in her. If another child pushed her over, she would not even try to get up. Lifelong malnutrition and abandonment had broken her spirit. She never spoke, never played, and never even cried. It was heartbreaking. I took a special interest in her and would try anything to get a response from her. Other children came to understand, too, that I would fight the fights for her that she lacked the strength to fight herself. After ridding her of worms and scabies and focusing attention on her, she eventually started to respond. It was a thrill just to see the occasional smile.

The nursing class was a major component of my goals for my year-long assignment. Before I'd even arrived, the orphanage administration selected twelve teenage girls to learn basic nursing skills in a class setting. By Bengali standards, they were quite grown up. The oldest girl, Rita, was my star student. She had lived nearly her entire life at the Children's Village. She was eager to impress me and learn. She was patient with my halting Bangla, and became a real friend to me as well. The nursing students and I met in one of the school classrooms a couple of times each week to learn basic physiology and first aid. The students would learn enough to act as nursing assistants at the clinic. They could take vital signs, change bandages, and do other tasks as supervised. Shyamoli, the nurse I worked with, helped me teach. We struggled to translate the material into Bangla. The girls all enjoyed the attention and lab time.

One Sunday at DICC, the international church, I met a British nurse who was working for an orphanage in the southern part of the country. Kathryn Beattie was my age and doing the same type of job as I was. We were both trying to learn orphanage care, clinic possibilities, and how to manage as a single woman in our respective settings. It was a treat when we could get together to talk in English and learn from each other's experiences. While she was in Dhaka for language school, we spent some weekends together. I also met an Australian family at church. They lived in Savar village. The husband taught at a Bible school. Occasionally, they invited me for a meal. The mother was a doctor; though she was not practicing medicine at the time, she answered questions for me as I needed guidance. She was an important part of helping me through those months.

Homesickness was still an occasional frustration despite my sincere joy in being allowed to do exactly what I had always dreamed of doing. I had rather hoped being prepared for Bangladesh and, indeed, being in love with it would exclude me from homesickness. It was a surprise and a disappointment to find that I still had some of the same struggles as many other missionaries.

One day when I was feeling sad, Shyamoli asked me what my favorite thing about Bangladesh was. I had kept it to myself, but I did have a top-shelf favorite thing I had found in Bangladesh. I shared my secret, not knowing how quickly she would spread the word. One little girl, Shamimara "Depa" Begum, was far and above what had touched my heart the most in Bangladesh. It made me smile every time I thought of her.

Depa was the youngest girl at the orphanage. She slept in a single bed with four other little girls on the top floor of the girls' building. Once I told Shyamoli my favorite "thing," within minutes Depa was brought in and placed on my desk in the clinic. She was told in ways she clearly understood that she was highly favored. I never planned to release that information, believing that living at an orphanage one really shouldn't have a favorite child any more than a mother should. Now everyone knew, and things changed because of it. At prayer time, Depa was confident that her rightful place was right in my lap, and she made sure everyone understood. The other children would generally leave a space. If they didn't leave her a space, she would come and boot them off. I used to hold her and sing a song I knew she couldn't understand. I sang to the tune of "All to Jesus I Surrender," telling her I would do anything for her, but knowing I really was more limited than that. She just enjoyed being loved. Every Wednesday night, we would all watch *MacGyver* on BTV, with Depa right on my lap.

Shyamoli was a prominent figure in my daily life. She spoke English fairly well—at least better than most—as it was her fourth language. She was from the Garo tribe in Bangladesh. We managed comical communication that brought us both endless amusement. On a rickshaw ride with her one day, I exclaimed, "The sky is so beautiful today." She replied, "You like the sky? Never mind. You take the sky. Okay." I taped our conversation one day, explaining that I wanted to take it home and share what fun discussions we had. When I demonstrated the recording process, she proceeded to take the microphone from me and say, "Hello, hello?... But they didn't answer." When I laughed, she would just smile because I was happy.

Shyamoli was married and had a beautiful daughter named Brishti. Her husband, Prodip, also worked for International Needs in the printing ministry. I went to her house for a Bengali holiday similar to Thanksgiving. Prodip was excited to have me come and experience the equivalent of carving "the turkey." The turkey, however, was a turtle. I had left my own pet tortoise, Sultan, at home with my sister. It was a joyous day with Shymoli and her family, but that part was hard to watch.

One day Shymoli came to work looking upset. I learned her unhappiness stemmed from discovering she was pregnant. She had decided to have an abortion, because they were planning to wait a while before having another child. I talked to her about the child being a gift from God and her decision to terminate the pregnancy because she thought God's timing was not right. Later, after she had the baby, I asked her what made her decide to keep her precious son, Shobuj. She stated it was because I had told her to. It turned out that directive came with quite a few responsibilities, which really I was glad to take on.

> If the Himalayas are the doorway to heaven,
> Bangladesh lies prostrate knocking at the doors
> of heaven.
>> —unknown

CHAPTER 5

Home in a Hurry

for i know the plans i have for you, says
the lord, plans to prosper you and not
to harm you, plans to give you a hope
and a future.

—Jeremiah 29:11

The political situation in Bangladesh was increasingly tumultuous. The US State Department recommended evacuation of nonessential Americans. I knew all along I was being watched over by my heavenly Father and never felt great personal risk; however, it wouldn't have been unreasonable to feel threatened.

Leaving seemed the only reasonable thing to do. In the late fall of 1990, the Persian Gulf crisis—Operation Desert Shield— was quickly becoming the first Gulf War. Bangladesh, being a Muslim nation, had many supporters of Iraq. Some of these supporters were marching down the street I lived on beating on drums and chanting, "Kill the American." As I was the only American in the area, not much mystery shrouded who the target was. Not only was it unsafe for me, my presence made life tenuous and dangerous for the staff and orphans at the Children's Village.

An imminent risk existed of people knocking down the wall around the orphanage in order to harm me. I was considered a guest, and in Bengali culture it would have been impolite to ask me to leave. Primarily for the sake of the safety of the children, I offered to leave the country. At first, I thought of going to India for a bit and letting the situation resolve. When it became clear the situation would not calm down soon, I purchased a return ticket to Seattle.

The military was in power again in Bangladesh, and at one point we were limited by round-the-clock curfews. Violence raged across the country. Daily life was ruled by political strikes, called hartals.* Productive life was curtailed. I had long-standing errands that needed to be done before I left Savar. Even if I could have gotten to Dhaka safely, the bank, embassies, and postal services were all risky places. The US Embassy had become a fortress. Americans had to get registered so the Embassy could contact us, if needed, for immediate evacuations or state department warnings. Without an American passport, it was difficult for people to even come close to the building. In Bangladesh, there were always many people trying to find entry into the promised land of America. The looks could kill as you flashed your American passport to get through the fortress doors.

Things were no easier out at the Village. I had come to feel like a prisoner on the orphanage compound. Jennie Richardson, my Australian doctor friend, lived close by, but I was never allowed outside the walls of the compound alone. Occasionally, I was allowed to visit in a rickshaw with a staff member riding a bicycle alongside me. The staff member would go and talk to the Richardsons before I got out of the rickshaw. The Richardsons would have me spend a few hours with them and then return me to the orphanage in their car. Some of these measures were

International Needs trying to keep me safe and some were just control issues. The director was frustrated by my independence—not a trait of most Bengali women. I was frustrated and getting more homesick dealing with the restrictions and rules of both the mission and the nation.

The continual lack of privacy also was wearing on me more and more as time went by. I had just one room on the orphanage compound with a couple of windows in it. Anytime I wasn't out with the children, they just stared at me through the windows—even if I was in the bathroom. They couldn't see into the high window, but they were still asking me questions and whistling for my attention.

Bangladesh is the most densely populated agrarian country in the world; there is hardly a need for the word "alone" in the Bengali vocabulary. In a sermon at Dhaka International Christian Church one Friday, the Pastor Cody Watson taught about three things that you cannot do alone: (1) be married, (2) be saved, and (3) go for a walk in Bangladesh.

I dearly loved the children, but I longed for some quiet and solitude at times. Sometimes to burn off nervous energy, I would move the table in my little room and jump rope for exercise. I ran hundreds of tight laps around the room and did push-ups to failure.

Many times, I wished I could have a few minutes alone. Monica Didi was always in my shadow. Sometimes I regretted having invited her in the room with me. She would occasionally ask if she could visit her home, which was just down the road. I would insist that she go and spend the night as well. I assured her I could manage breakfast on my own and that she could stay until lunch at least. Hers was one of the few Bengali houses I went to during my stay in Savar. She knew exactly how hot I liked my curry. It was having my same food only at her house instead of mine.

Despite some struggles in Bangladesh, I was so sad to leave. When it was time, Shyamoli thought it amusing to encourage me to take Depa with me. I would have loved to, but it was really not possible. It was not legal to adopt Bengali children, and I was young and single at the time. Depa crawled into my trunk and smiled. It broke my heart to leave her, but I promised I would be back. I knew I wasn't done in Bangladesh.

I had to be taken out of the orphanage compound lying flat on the floor in the back of the van under the cover of darkness. The International Needs driver navigated the blockades and ferried me quickly to Dhaka's Zia airport for my escape.

Holding Depa at the Children's Village

I looked into the adoption process once I was back at home and was told that I should wait to apply because I was too young to be applying as a single person for an independent overseas international adoption. I hung a big picture of Depa at the head of my futon. I cried myself to sleep for months missing them all so badly. A few months later, my separation was even harder. A cyclone hit the coast of Bangladesh in April 1991, killing 150,000 people in one day. I had been in the flood in 1988 and knew I could help, but the war in the Middle East was fully in progress. I was out four-wheeling in my Jeep back in Washington when the breaking news came on: "This just in … 'Operation Desert Shield' is now 'Operation Desert Storm.'" I prayed, cried, and fasted … and it wasn't long before the Lord again flexed and poured out His blessings to give me the desires of my heart again in the most exciting way.

> I will come again with love to these rivers and
> fields, to this land of Bangla, to its sorrowful green
> shores washed by the waves of the Jalangi River.
> —Rabindranath Tagore

CHAPTER 6

An Extra Clinic, 1991

but seek first his kingdom and his
righteousness and all these things will
be added to you as well.
—matthew 6:33

After I had been back in the States only a few months, Kathryn Beattie—the British nurse from the other orphanage in Bangladesh—came to America to work at a Christian camp in Cape Cod, Massachusetts, for the summer. We had kept in touch since our time together in Bangladesh. When she arrived, I telephoned from Seattle to chat. Kate was at Camp Good News, directed by Faith Willard, founder of the mission organization Kate worked with in Bangladesh. The mission, known in the States as the Widow's Friend, was started in partnership with Camp Good News in Forestdale, Massachusetts.

After the war for independence, Bangladesh was firmly rooted in the unenviable position of being the poorest nation in the world. Many widows and children were starving in the aftermath of the war. In an attempt to help this situation, the godly family that ran Camp Good News opened an orphanage in Bangladesh.

When Kate and I first met, she was on her way to their Home of Joy in the southwestern part of Bangladesh.

While Kate and I were reminiscing, Faith Willard got on the phone, too, and asked if I was interested in coming to work at Camp Good News as well. If so, she said she would send me an application. She also mentioned the Bangladesh project. I wasn't looking for a job at the time. My boss had just recommended that I apply for the assistant nurse manager position on the cardiac floor at Harborview Medical Center back in Seattle. A few minutes later, Faith picked up the phone again while Kate and I were still talking and said she would just mail me information and an application. As Kate and I continued talking, Faith briefly interrupted the conversation a third time. She told me to forget the application process at all. The job was mine. Long story made short, I resigned from my job at Harborview again and left for Cape Cod for a summer of camp nursing.

This was really a time of testing each other for the possibility of serving together in Bangladesh. Working as a nurse at Camp Good News for the summer was a great experience. I even got a bonus friend in the deal, a Bangladeshi daughter of a general, who was feeling fairly lost in America. It was the fifth camp I had worked at over the years. Camp work was something I always enjoyed. The pre-camp Bible teaching was conducted by retired missionary friends of Faith's, Patricia and Hazel St. John. As Christian camp experiences can be, this was an encouraging and faith-building mountaintop summer. Some East Coast camps differ from those in the western United States in that the campers come for the whole summer, not just for a week. The campers and staff represented a culturally diverse mix. Many were from New York City, some from the various parts of the United States, and others from around the globe.

Driving around the United States in my Jeep was grand fun too. When I informed my parents that I would be quitting at Harborview to go to Massachusetts, my surprised mom asked if she could ride along to see the country with me. It was no leisurely drive, but I planned the route to afford myself the most opportunities to see my own nation. Mom and I enjoyed visiting Yellowstone, Mount Rushmore, the Great Lakes, Niagara Falls, and more, even though we spent only thirty minutes at some of the magnificent sites. My mom was able to enjoy Camp Good News as well for a few days before returning to Spokane on a plane from Boston. We had a fun-filled, memory-making time together, which we revel in still.

I took a longer, more relaxed drive on my way back home. Kate accompanied me to tour America before her return to England. We drove through the Rockies, Grand Canyon, and even went to Disneyland. While enjoying all of America, we discussed Bangladesh. She had struggled tremendously, as I had in Savar, and was not returning. For me, however, plans were in motion to go back. I wanted to learn from her what it would be like living at Home of Joy and serving with "Friends of Bangladesh," as Faith Willard's group was known there. This would be my third venture into Bangladesh. Amazingly, God had arranged them all. I never even applied to any mission there or for any position. As promised in Ephesians 2:10, these were the good works that He had prepared in advance for me to do.

Besides the excitement of anticipating my return to Bangladesh, God had made it even sweeter for me. Shortly after telling Starla my plans, she asked if I would consider her joining me. Starla and I had a great adventure in 1990 touring India and Thailand together before she went to Savar to see where I would be working. In the meantime, God had been working in her heart. Starla had decided after her trip that she would consider missions herself. She felt nervous even to ask, but told me that she'd thought, *"Why not just go with Jill?"* She certainly had no reason to be nervous. I was ecstatic at the prospect of her joining me. We prepared together again. She planned to go for a year this time—and oh, the plans God had in store. Her companionship would make my time less difficult with homesickness issues. Not many friendships are bonded the way ours would be that year. We launched into 1992, a year literally filled with saving each other's lives again and again.

Good-byes are very painful in the world of missions. My parents struggled, as did my dear sister Valerie. They were all there, with many teary others, seeing us off from Sea-Tac Airport. I could barely look at my sister as the tears rolled freely down our faces. Valerie pulled Starla aside to beg her to take care of me.

Starla and I made the long journey right after Christmas and arrived in time to start the new term at language school. We started a three-month-long language training course right away to learn Bengali at HEED (Health, Education, Economic Development) language school. We stayed just a few blocks away at the Friends of Bangladesh (FOB) national director's house. Starla and I made ourselves a part of the Hubert Gomes family, partly at their insistence. Not only did they feed us, but his wife, Suzanne, taught us to cook Bengali food. To be respectful, we called her *mashi,*★ which means *auntie.* Once while Starla was in the tiny kitchen talking to mashi, I wandered in and thanked Starla again for being with me. I gave her a wee kiss on the cheek. Mashi got a look on her face and groaned, "Jill loves you, but she doesn't love me." I then kissed her too, and that became the standard of how we greeted one another in the house.

The Gomeses's young son, Paul, was deaf. Starla could communicate with him better than most as she had been an interpreter for a church for the hearing impaired in Seattle. While the Gomes family opened up Bangladesh to us, we helped make the world bigger for them too. Some of the other FOB missionaries were surprised to see Mr. Gomes act so differently with us than he had with them. He was not at all uptight at home, but joked and conversed warmly.

When Starla and I got an apartment of our own, we invited the Gomeses to come join us for a homemade American meal. They came two hours early to watch we what made and see how we would do it differently than they were used to. *Mashi* was full of laughter in our presence.

We'd spend mornings at school and afternoons studying, playing cards, visiting, and helping as much as we could at some of the Friends of Bangladesh projects. I had so many things I wanted to do and accomplish that it was hard for me to have to slow down and do the language course first.

Despite what seemed like slow living in March 1992, I came down with typhoid fever in my third module at language school. At this point, I wasn't even living in the more remote parts of Bangladesh. I was sorely disappointed to have typhoid get in my way and slow me down so much. Typhoid is a miserable disease. Every afternoon, my fever would go a degree higher than it had the day before. Every part of my body hurt. Despite a fever of 106 degrees, I had a slow heart rate—not much circulatory support. I remember being in tears at the pain of so little circulation to my extremities. I had clear blue lines on both arms and legs every day at the point where the blood flow shut down. The pain was excruciating. Though my body was burning hot, my limbs were ice cold. With weather in the nineties, I was dressed for winter in my room. This was, however, the first time in three years that I didn't have diarrhea (and the only time over the course of nine whole years). After two weeks of antibiotics and rest, the fever abated. I got back to work as quickly as I could. Starla and I then went to visit some language school friends in the peaceful setting of the Sylhet tea gardens for a rest. Just escaping the Dhaka urban chaos was a breath of fresh air, literally and figuratively.

I missed most of the third module at language school and never learned Bangla writing very well. That turned out to be the end of my formal Bangla training, but God was more than faithful. The Bangla language came as a gift, given to me by God, that went hand in hand with my love for the Bengali people. I eventually spoke Bangla well enough to manage phone calls without people knowing I was a *bideshi*,★ a foreigner.

An early phone call attempt while living with the Gomes family was not as successful. I answered the phone and then did not understand a single word coming through the receiver. I hurriedly motioned for the house help girl to come take over the phone call. Elora took the phone, listened briefly, and then promptly hung up. She asked, irritated, why I had given the phone to her. Ashamed, I hated to admit that I understood nothing that was said. She informed me it was an obscene phone call. I never did learn any of those words.

While the language came fairly easily to me, not everything did. I was at language school with a couple of other women who became close friends. We were all adjusting to Bangladesh together. Randa, another Friends of Bangladesh missionary, could wear a sari so beautifully and she could eat any kind of food the Bengalis would serve her, but for a long time her Bangla was not as smooth as mine. Nan, a Baptist friend, spoke Bengali like a poet and dressed elegantly in a sari, but she couldn't stand even the smell of rice at the time—let alone curry. I could speak well and eat any tuber or fish head, but I hated dressing up. It would take me forty-five minutes to put on a sari. When I would appear, people would want to "fix" me. I found saris frustrating, so I rarely dressed very Bengali.

Though I had been to Bangladesh a couple of times before, this was the first time I was really trying to assimilate in many cultural aspects. Much more adjusting needed to be done. Having lived with all those orphans before and not having gone to proper language school, I had a functional, but grammatically poor Bangla base. Not surprisingly, I was told I spoke like a five-year-old village orphan—like Depa.

The thrill of having a clinic to start was not conducive to resting much after typhoid. I was making plans for the Tilok village clinic at Home of Joy orphanage in southwestern Bangladesh. Starla and I were also helping at the FOB clinic in the enormous Old Dhaka slum, primarily to get a good knowledge base for running the future clinic out in the countryside.

While we were occupied with that, the Presbyterian mission asked if FOB could take over their longtime clinic in the slum north of the capital in Tongi. When Friends of Bangladesh went to procure government permission, we were advised not to locate our clinic in that area at all. Tongi boasted a large slum of eighteen thousand people in less than two square miles. Known to be full of miscreants and criminals, it also hosted the site of the second largest Muslim gathering in the world, behind only the hajj.★ Once a year, buses are crowded to near toppling, overloaded with people going to worship out in Gazipur at the big mosque. I systematically did a thorough community survey in preparation for taking over the facility from the Presbyterians. Obviously, the needs extended beyond just healthcare, so despite the government home office recommendations, the Friends of Bangladesh NGO forged ahead with plans to continue the clinic.

Starla and Jill at the Tongi Clinic

We again saw the Lord move mightily in Tongi. Our hand-chosen workers shone as beacons in our new community. About one-half of the staff was Muslim and the other half Christian. All were invited to come to morning prayers and devotions, and all were loved with the love of the Lord regardless of religion. The clinic had been running at a high level for nearly twenty years. On Thursday, it closed with sixty staff; on the following Sunday, it opened with only twelve.

To transition the clinic, I did a lot of behind-the-scenes prework. It would be regrettable to lose such a great clinic, so we needed to be sure that most needs could still be met. I went through the slum and through all the clinic records to try to find what the patterns showed we needed most. To make the big cutback work out for the bulk of the community, we focused the clinic efforts on diarrheal diseases, tuberculosis,★ prenatal care, nutrition-related illnesses, and a health education department. We still managed to see over 150 patients a day, even after cutting so many services.

We hired some lovely Bengali nurses and two health educators, Lutfanessa and Rabia. They taught in the waiting area while people were at the clinic. Starla wrote a fantastic play, in Bangla, teaching about worms. It was called the *Crimi* (pronounced creamy) *Bahini*, or *Worm Fighters*. The drama was well received as being entertaining and educational and also showing great respect for the beloved Mukti Bahini freedom fighters. It also played to the Bengali's love of the beautiful rhyming lilt of their language. Lal Chan's daily job was sweeping and hand-pumping water to the roof tanks so we would have some running water. It was a terrible and hard job, but in Bangladesh, even those are hard to get. He went about it gladly and served as an integral part of the new clinic team. Even though he was Muslim, he recognized that the Christian missionaries were different. Everyone was respected and fully included.

Our watchman, Mohammed (Md.) Hassan, made a great choice for guard because everyone was afraid of him and were inclined to do what he said; however, that had a downside. He claimed too much power and authority and was robbing the mission in several areas. One example was when he connected illegally to our power lines and then sold connections for electricity throughout the slum at our expense. Later, we realized he was stealing embroidery pieces from the women's sewing center as well. When it was discovered we were short on nakshi★

embroidery pieces, Hassan was interrogated and then cautiously fired. His argument was that if he couldn't work at the clinic, then nobody else could either. He threatened to cut the Achilles tendons of anyone caught walking to work there. For weeks, we had to exercise caution. We staggered our start and stop times so we would not have predictable work patterns. Bricks were thrown at the mission van. Everyone was intimidated and fearful. The whole community experienced answered prayer right along with us through the painful process. It was a scary time, but God was faithful.

An example of faithfulness to us all during this trial was our semiretired missionary, Dr. Herbert Coddington. The reason the clinic was offered to us was because of dear Dr. Coddington. He had actually started the clinic years before when he was serving in Bangladesh with the Presbyterian mission. Now that he was with Friends of Bangladesh, they looked to us when they had to relinquish the clinic to move to their newly built facility. Dr. Coddington was widely revered in the area. He had retired but couldn't tolerate not serving the Lord on the mission field, so he would make trips from his North Carolina home for short periods to help in the clinics and share the gospel.

Dr. Coddington was white haired and fragile. His years of cutting-edge medicine were long past. He had graduated from Cornell so long ago that nearly every medicine we used was new since then. He'd had many years' experience as a tuberculosis specialist. He had done such treatments as collapsing a lung and filling the cavity with ping pong balls or clipping the phrenic nerve to give the lung complete rest for a year. Despite his forgetfulness, at the clinic all the patients "needed" to see Dr. Coddington. When I triaged patients, I would try to direct some of the sickest patients in to see our

Bengali physician, Dr. Biswas. He complained, "I would give them the best medicine, and they would not be satisfied. Dr. Coddington, however, could give them a glass of water, and they would be delighted."

Though Dr. Coddington was older to the point of being forgetful, he always remembered to tell his patients of God's love. He rode around on a motorcycle handing out tracts throughout Dhaka in the early morning hours each day. One morning, he crashed his motorcycle and then just stuck a piece of toilet paper over the resulting gash in his arm. He would forget to eat, so we younger missionaries would often invite him for meals—both because we loved him and worried about him. When some trouble surfaced for facilitating a Bible study in the Tongi slum, the leaders at the home department asked us why we couldn't all be more like Dr. Coddington. We assured the Bangladeshi government officials that we would try to be just like him.

We loved to ask Dr. Coddington what time it was. Even though he was in Bangladesh, he kept his watch on North Carolina time. As he gazed at his watch, he would get absolutely lost. Looking surprised, he would say, "Oh look, it's noon back in NC. Paige [his wife, who no longer traveled with him] is just sitting down to lunch." He was a grandfather to us all and taught us well while keeping us amused with his Bangla—spoken with a Carolina southern drawl.

The Friends of Bangladesh mission had several projects in the Dhaka area, and Starla and I tried to be involved in all we could. Our main objective was the orphanage in the south of the country, but while we were in Dhaka we were an active part of the FOB team.

Besides the clinic in Tongi, two other Friends of Bangladesh projects shared the same compound. One, the Widows' Sewing

Center, employed two hundred women who sewed *nakshi kantha*,★ a national handicraft of Bangladesh. They are gorgeous silk on silk embroidery pieces with Bible verses or pictures depicting life in Bangladesh. This was the first project the mission started after the 1971 war, when so many widows were left unable to provide for themselves. After some women were found to be hearing impaired, Miss Cho, from Korea, opened a school for them. She shared the love of the Lord while she opened up their world.

The Tongi clinic was not the first clinic for FOB. In Dhaka's old city, the Telagu Clinic served the poorest of the poor right near the largest slum in this megacity of nearly ten million people. Women in Bangladesh, especially at that time, had limited opportunities. So, FOB organized a boarding house where they could live. Many would otherwise have not been able to go to school or work. Friends of Bangladesh was a small mission, but we were a tight-knit group. We worked to support each other with the goals of each of the various projects.

Working at the Tongi clinic was delaying my move to the Home of Joy orphanage in Tilok village, outside Khulna in the southwest part of the country. At the clinic, it was widely known that the orphanage was where I had come to serve. One family in the slum decided I was the obvious solution to their problem—and mine. One day when I arrived at the clinic, a surprise was waiting for me: a twelve-year-old local boy with severe spinal tuberculosis. His family was unable to give him the care he needed. They reasoned that if they brought Delwar "Dilu" Hossein to me, that I would ferry him right to the orphanage where he would be cared for. They were wrong. Home of Joy was not keen to introduce TB to the facility. I arranged for a place for Dilu to stay in the slum, his new home in his same old neighborhood. Having him stay with an older lady, they both got a family as well as having their food and essential needs met. His tuberculosis was treated and plans were made to take him to the orphanage when he was no longer infectious.

Dilu was my shadow anytime I was at the Tongi slum. If he showed up early in the morning, I would march him right back to school. I had to sign all his schoolwork. By introducing adequate nutrition, I tried to induce a growth spurt while he was under treatment for curing the tuberculosis. It worked to a degree. He grew a few inches and his spine straightened out a little. The best part was that growing stronger, smarter, and healthier paid off in a way we were too afraid even to hope for: his family came back to visit him at one point and decided to take him home.

Dilu and PhuPhu

I had seen spinal tuberculosis before, but my eyes were opened wider when Dilu dropped into my life. These tiny, hunched-over, broken children were often used for begging professionally. I began to see them everywhere and longed to reach out to them. My connection with Dilu connected me to all those children with spinal tuberculosis, creating a desire to gather them all into my care. I envisioned starting a home just for them with all the needed inpatient and outpatient treatments necessary to help them live a full life. They needed surgical, medical, nutritional, and educational support. Two full years of treatment and rest would give them the best chance for a cure. Unfortunately, to my knowledge, no such place exists in the world.

Traveling around Bangladesh was fraught with danger. A missionary friend, Bob McGurty, used to say, "One more coat of paint, and that would have been a hit." One day, Starla and I were riding in a baby taxi,★ the ubiquitous three-wheeled motor transport, on our way to a meeting about the Tongi Presbyterian clinic. I saw a car coming toward us but didn't even get excited. They always look like they were going to hit you—but usually they don't. This time was different. The car that looked as if it would hit the baby taxi did, in fact, collide with us.

I was ejected out the side of the car. Starla was battered, but not thrown out. The driver was crushed by the vehicle, which turned over onto his head. I was bleeding profusely and couldn't see anything at all because my glasses were broken on impact. As I screamed unintelligibly, Starla jumped out of the baby taxi and ran to me. She wrapped her arms around me and prayed. While we had been in India the year before, her dear friend back at home had been killed in a car accident just two weeks after getting married. Starla heard me panicking and decided that all she couldn't do for Jennifer was not going to be repeated with me.

The baby taxi driver looked as if he might die. We put money into his pocket for expenses and paid another driver to take him to a local hospital, but we never learned what became of him. The car that hit us followed the usual Bangladesh traffic accident protocol, which is to "abscond" from the scene. In America, we call it a hit-and-run.

We were bruised, bloodied, and sore—and late to the meeting. I stopped at the Gomeses' home on the way to the meeting to quickly clean off the blood. For weeks, Starla had to be careful not to make me laugh too much. For a long time, I didn't know why it hurt so badly. Later I learned my ribs broke when I was thrown onto the road.

> I used to ask God to help me. Then I asked if I might help Him. I ended up by asking Him to do his work through me.
>
> —Hudson Taylor[4]

CHAPTER 7

A New Orphanage

let the little children come to me, and
do not hinder them, for the kingdom of
heaven belongs to such as these.
—matthew 19:14

I traveled to the Home of Joy orphanage as often as I could. The Tongi clinic and typhoid kept delaying me from moving there. Down in the village, the children were waiting for me to come. A whole new clinic was yet to be initiated. After language school, I was back and forth for six months between Dhaka and the orphanage before starting to settle there. The HOJ orphanage was much different from the one I served at in Savar. The fifty-six children had better supervision and sanitation. But just like in Savar, many children touched my life.

The adjacent village of Tilok was also worlds apart from Savar. Local people were not as accustomed to seeing foreigners. A ferry crossing was necessary to get across the Rupsha River. At the ferryghat,* people would crowd around my car and stare in the windows, pointing and talking. Later, they would become used to my driving around and being a constant presence.

The mission had to make a road to the orphanage in order to build on the site. The orphanage was actually the only *pucca* (substantially built structure) in the village. All the homes were made of mud and straw. Building the clinic served two purposes: helping our neighbors and providing opportunities to get involved in their lives.

In October 1992, FOB was blessed to be involved in a rescue operation of seventeen little Bangladeshi boys that catapulted me to more permanent residence at Home of Joy. They boys, aged three to seven, had been kidnapped for use as camel jockeys in the United Arab Emirates. A Bangladeshi professor working in the United States contacted Faith, who was then back in Massachusetts, after he had seen the news. Knowing she had resources back in Bangladesh, he asked her about getting the boys repatriated. It was a complicated, many months long process that brought Friends of Bangladesh a lot of publicity.

We called them the "Bombay boys," as that is where they were found through a tip to the Indian police. Many of them were so young when they were kidnapped out of Bangladesh that they had not yet learned to speak. They had just been learning Bangla when they were taken away to a place where Hindi was spoken. After nearly a year in India, many had learned some Hindi before they were abruptly brought back to Bangladesh. They were old enough to comprehend, but they had no language skills. In fact, they shared a sort of private language all their own. Lokman, about four, was the most vocal. He would mimic everybody's movements and vocal inflections, and then he would try to communicate using these tools. He would "talk" using proper enough inflection that it seemed we should understand it. He would shake his fingers, put his hands on his hips, and then grunt a question. It was so frustrating for him that nobody could answer his unending questions.

The boys had been frightened, mistreated, and sequestered together. We had prepared two rooms with beds and staff for the anticipated twenty-five boys. In the end, only seventeen got to return to Bangladesh. The remaining eight were claimed to be the children of the kidnappers and were kept in India by the police. The seventeen scared little boys flew together on a plane with Faith and were met at Zia airport by a bus sent to bring them to the orphanage. All were sick, undernourished, and terrified. Upon arrival at the orphanage, they panicked about being separated into two rooms, even though they were on the same floor with just a dining room between them. They preferred to stack into bed together than the further trauma of separation.

The whole FOB/ Home of Joy staff, including myself, took care of them physically and tried to soothe their deep emotional wounds. The press visited to photograph them and spread the pictures all over the nation. It took nearly a year, but fourteen of the seventeen were reunited with their families. It was difficult yet rewarding work, heartbreaking and fulfilling at the same time.

The first boy went home after only a few months. It took several more months before the next family was found, and four were turned over to their families on that same day. I was glad to be in the States later when the rest of the emotional returns occurred. So many of the boys did not remember their families and screamed with terror at being taken away again. The remaining three were eventually transferred to a government facility when their families could not be located. We were grateful for the time we were able to share with them.

The Bombay boys were not the only ones who were broken. Every child at an orphanage has issues with abandonment on some level. Many had watched their families die. Some had just been abandoned or left at the local hospital. A few baby girls were found left in the city dump. Some newborn girls were left in discarded powdered milk tins. Martha was found in a field as a day-old baby. Bipul was handed to the *chowkidar* (watchman) at UNICEF by his single mother, who said she would be right back—but did not return for him. Sonali was left alone at the train station as a toddler. One baby girl was abandoned at the nearby jute mill. Local people or missionaries would route the babies to Home of Joy. Infants who had been abandoned had an easier time adjusting than those who remembered life with a family. Stories of parents dying and family trying to care for them until they couldn't anymore were heartrending enough, but then came the trauma of being left in an orphanage to experience loss all over again. All the HOJ children were special, of course. Faith called them her cherubs. The number of stories of desperation matched the number of precious children in our care.

One little girl was brought in after both her parents had died. The neighbor who brought her said she was about four months old. She weighed barely four pounds and was very near death. I named her Hope. Indeed I hoped and prayed that somehow she would make it. I immediately rushed her to Khulna for a chest X-ray. The double pneumonia discovered was critically life threatening. Her lung and growth problems continued. She was on and off antibiotics, steroids, inhalers, and chest physiotherapy for the next year. God was faithful again and certainly gave all of us at Home of Joy the desires of our hearts. Hope stayed small, but she met her developmental milestones and grew up with the rest of kids.

The orphanage buildings were divided into family units with up to ten children per room with a mashi (room mother). A few biological sibling units were in the home, but all the children considered themselves family. The outside "friends" they had were other children from the United States who wrote to them and prayed for them. This was one of the ministries through Camp Good News. Papri, Labio, and China were biological siblings; although they welcomed all the other children, they kept a special watch over each other. Konika and Lotika grew up at HOJ and did not consider each other any more a sibling than all the others. In keeping with expectations, the girls more than twice outnumbered the boys. The older ones helped to care for the younger ones. Even without real parents, the children were greatly cherished.

Though they were easy to love, it should be no surprise that they were not always cherubs. Besides being the nurse for HOJ, my tasks included spiritual mentor, teacher, game player, swimming instructor, and also administrator. The often unpleasant task of being the disciplinarian for them all was also added to my job description. They had plenty of naughty days. Once, Moshe and Arun were playing with matches. They didn't want to get caught, so they threw the evidence over the compound wall. Unfortunately, that set the neighbor's chicken coop on fire—not a good way to be a "light" of the gospel for our Hindu neighbors.

Though the children were regularly and adequately fed, stealing food from the kitchen was common. Piku got into the red chilies and made a fine mash, which she discarded to avoid punishment. In school that morning, she kept shaking her hands wildly and rubbing her face. She had to come clean to be able to get help for the burning sensation hurting her hands and eyes from the hot chili oil. That was more than punishment enough. Most of their infractions were like those of all brothers and sisters, simple disagreements and occasional fisticuffs.

Once when the children were practicing marching to music, they pushed the orphanage's van out of the way. Eight-year-old Labio jumped up on the back bumper to ride while it was being pushed. Of course, he fell off. The back wheels of the van rolled right over his upper leg and broke the ball right off his femur. The school principal came to wake me from a nap to say that Labio had been run over. I pictured him putting his foot under the wheel, but Boby, our music teacher, was insistent that I look at him immediately. I was dumbfounded seeing how badly he had been run over. I slid a large piece of wood under him to keep him lying flat and put him into the van from the back, still lying on the plywood. We went straight to the X-ray shop before taking patient and the radiographs to the Shishu (Children's) Hospital in Khulna.

The doctor there began casting the whole leg, right to the top of the thigh. I questioned how that was supposed to help, considering the fracture was above that point. Then they hooked him up to traction and said I could take him back to the orphanage. I explained that traction with a brick hanging off the end of a bunk bed was not going to work in a children's home. It was twenty pounds of traction now, but once some little kid came swinging off the end of it, the traction would be changed beyond reasonable limits.

Labio stayed in the Khulna Children's Hospital, with his mashi, for two weeks. I brought him back on the plywood in a spica cast that went from below his knee up to his armpits. Shortly after arriving back at home, he managed to pry the metal bar out and was trying to walk, still in a spica cast. After a couple more weeks, I removed the whole cast so he didn't get a head injury to complicate the situation. Labio quickly healed and was up to full speed within a couple of months.

Suturing was a much-needed skill. I received extra training before departing, so I could handle it myself. I didn't do much of it, however, despite having brought all the necessary supplies. Often, it was our own orphanage kids who needed the sutures. I found that I wanted to be the one to hold them and tell them it would be all right. Five-year-old Rajiv was so excited when they changed rooms one day that he did a flying leap off the top bunk and sustained a serious gash to the head that needed stitches. He was inconsolable. Instead of holding him down to do it myself, I took him up the road to a man who did suturing out of a little shop. I handed him the appropriate sterile needle and thread. He proceeded to put the suture material right into his mouth like people often do when they are going to thread a needle. I stopped him on the spot, gave him another sterile supply and told him *not* to put it in his mouth this time. After the first stitch, he instructed our driver to put his thumb over the wound to hold pressure before he got the next one in—and before I could stop him. I held Rajiv in my arms. I treated him with antibiotics once we were back at the orphanage to stave off infection.

Leya was about seven and was constantly having bad ear infections. Since Starla and I made frequent trips back and forth from Khulna to Dhaka, we decided to take Leya with us once and arranged to have her tonsils removed. She thought it would be so thrilling to go to the capital and have a grand adventure, even if it meant she had to have surgery. She seemed so excited to taste the exotic life outside the orphanage. When the airplane ascended, however, she was already reconsidering. "Auntie, are those clouds out the window?" She held my hand with a white-knuckle grip.

Back at our apartment in Dhaka, we went down for dinner with the Walter family. There was Jell-o on the table and Leya was in tears again, saying, "I am Bengali. I eat rice." When bedtime came, we put two mattresses on the floor. Starla, Leya, and I slept all together in our room. We hardly let go of hands for the whole trip. In Dhaka, the ENT surgeon who was to do the operation examined her in his office first. When I took her to the hospital, staff asked who would be staying with her and taking care of her. In Bangladesh, family members take care of the hospitalized patients. I explained that, as she was an orphan, I was her only family and planned to stay with her myself. We lived in an apartment on the second floor of Dr. Dave and Nan Walters house, who were doing two years of language study. When I explained to the surgeon that our house in Dhaka had two nurses and a doctor, he agreed to let me take Leya home right after surgery. I carried her out to a baby taxi in my arms while she was still asleep from anesthesia. Leya stayed in Dhaka with us for ten days. She visited the zoo and several national sites, but she was more than relieved to return to the orphanage.

It was night when we crossed the Rupsha River to get to our village on the other side of the river. I took a local public transport called a *vangari*★ to get to Tilok. It is like a bicycle rickshaw but with a wooden platform on the back instead of a two-seat bench. As we bounced along, a man also on the vangari grabbed my breast and tried to make some moves, all while I had Leya in my lap. I felt threatened and even more protective of my young charge. I grabbed the man's arm, much to his surprise, and pulled it up behind his neck. In fact, much to my own surprise, I offered in Bangla to break his arm. He apologized and said it was an "accident." At that point, I smashed the side of his head with my umbrella. What a relief that he and the other men all ran away. Leya was not even aware what had happened. I didn't fall apart until after I got her safely and happily back to the Home of Joy, where she had tales of her adventures to tell.

On another trip to Dhaka, somebody brought a young boy, who looked to be about six years old, to our apartment. He was alone on the streets of Dhaka with no family. He had no idea where he came from or if he had any connections anywhere. He knew only that his name was Liton. After some futile searching, we decided that the orphanage was the best place for him. He had never been to school. Liton turned out to be a tough little guy. Having to fend for himself for so long left him almost unable to accept help at all. He was a worker from the first day at the orphanage. We kept finding food in his bed all the time too; he was not at all confident that more food would be available later. When he got an ear infection, he didn't say anything at all about it. I just happened to notice blood coming out his ear and checked on it. The eardrum had ruptured, but he showed no signs of any feelings at all. He certainly did respond to love, but he thrived on the attention. After just a few months, we learned that he was not that young after all, but rather ten or eleven years old. He had been so poorly nourished, that he was lagging far behind in growth. He grew taller and stronger so quickly that we knew he had to be older, but school never did come easy to him.

I felt rather sorry for my own parents that it seemed they would never have grandchildren. So when another little girl was brought to me, I named her Kristine—as a granddaughter for my mother, or at least the best I could offer. Mom sponsored her, of course. I never anticipated marriage or the remote possibility of parenting at that point. That thought may have made me love "my" Bengali children all the more.

Annee Praying at Home of Joy

Annee was five years old when I arrived at Home of Joy. Her birth name was Hamida Khatun. She came to us from a Muslim family when she was younger than two. After her father died, her mother tried to care for her alone as best she could. She tied Annee to a bedpost when she went to work, leaving her a little food to get by. At some point, Annee's mom died too. The child was found home alone, tied to the end of a bed, starving and handicapped from being literally tethered all the time. When she was discovered and brought to the orphanage, she was a shell of sadness and devastation. Faith wondered if she would ever even try to get up and learn to walk.

As Annee grew in the Christ-filled environment, she met the Lord and was filled with His spirit. Annee knew Jesus in a way few people do. She was a "prayer warrior" at only five years old. When she prayed, it was as if the doors of heaven were pulled wide open and you could see God. If anyone at the orphanage wasn't feeling well, you would find Annee nearby—interceding unobtrusively. By just meeting her, she taught others about Christ. It was the desire of my heart to see God use Annee to further His kingdom in Bangladesh. It was her prayer to grow up to be a "Bible woman" and to share Christ in her own nation.

Even though I loved what I was doing, working in the orphanage was exhausting—physically, spiritually, and emotionally. I was back in Khulna shortly after round one with typhoid, and I relapsed the summer of 1992. By God's grace, Starla was with me. I credit God, using Starla, for my still being alive today. The typhoid relapse was different than the initial infection. Instead of not feeling well and getting a bit sicker each day, everything happened in a day, all at once. I had a headache in the morning. By afternoon, my temperature was 106.8 degrees and it just stayed that way. My Widal lab tests, to look for typhoid, were off the charts. I was obviously profoundly sick. When I made it to doctor in Khulna, he informed me I would die right away unless hospitalized. I replied that I would rather die at home than in their hospital. My hospital time in Kolkata had been enough of a third-world medicine experience for me.

Starla was shocked and terrified, but I persuaded her not to worry. I wasn't going to die at all—because I had *her*. Poor Starla, the pressure was on. I didn't leave the bedroom at all for a month. She ran intravenous fluids when I needed them and gave me antibiotics every day. I came mighty close to dying of typhoid. God's provision of Starla's loving care pulled me through, though dragged me through is a better description. I had about sloughed away my intestines and had to be on a *no* fiber diet for months. Visible and bleeding holes throughout my GI tract dotted from the back of my mouth to the other end. I became septic. Eventually, I was bleeding from everywhere: my tears, ears, nose, throat, urine, stool, and other little random sores. Every little scratch or sore ran with pus and blood. The fever was unrelenting. Starla prayed for me every time I closed my eyes. She prayed that I would get some rest and then, by God's mercy, be alive to open them again. When I would be tempted to get out of bed, she would bribe me gently with Scrabble or cribbage.

Being sick in the village was uncomfortable on many fronts. Everyone was full of "village" advice and warnings. I was told my sickness happened because I walked in the afternoon sun or because I showered after dark. By the time of my twenty-fifth birthday I had turned a corner and felt confident I would, in fact, live. We returned to Dhaka for some rest and celebrated my birthday with some friends who visited quietly while I lay on the couch.

The risk of death in Bangladesh is a real possibility. I honestly thought I would be dead by the time I was twenty-five. I was at peace with the idea if I could have the privilege of serving the Lord in Bangladesh. Seeing Bengalis kneel at the foot of the cross was what all my wildest dreams were made of. Who could ask for more than giving your life while realizing your dreams. Brother Andrew, famous for getting Bibles into difficult places, said, "There are no closed doors to the gospel, provided that, once you get inside, you don't care if you ever come out." Being told at twenty-four that I would die was not shocking, or even unexpected, for me. It was not even really a deterrent. After surviving the typhoid sepsis, in some ways I started feeling like a cat—with the whole nine lives thing. I was weak and tired but still so happy to be about the Lord's work in Bangladesh.

Starla and I worked together at everything, running back and forth across the country. It might seem like having two nurses, we could have accomplished more by splitting up, the better to divide and conquer. But we were known simply as "JillandStarla"—one word. We were strength for each other when we needed it. We were courage for each other at times when we needed that. I have said that Starla and I took turns saving each other's life. My role for her was support.

Shortly after we arrived, Starla began having nightmares that filled her with terror. We endured many sleepless, tear-filled nights. Bangladesh is a very spiritually dark place, and daily life can take all your coping skills and more. Anything you have "issues" with will absolutely come to the surface, because there is no chance of just gliding through. We discovered that God's motive for sending Starla to Bangladesh was, in part, to work in her heart as much as it was for her to help with His work on the other side of the world. I endured many hard days trying to be sure nothing would hurt her in any way. I was willing to stay up forever to watch her if that was necessary. The Walter family was also critical in holding her up. They partnered with me in watching and supporting her.

One night, I called to America to talk to our roommate and dear friend, Cindy. I told her to be in prayer for Starla and then called, "Hey, Starla, Cindy is on the phone." Understand this was before cell phones, texting, and other forms of communication were the norm, as they are now. I tried to call my parents about once every three months to let them know I was okay up to that minute. This phone call could cost a hundred dollars for just a short visit. Otherwise, our cost of living was only a few hundred dollars a month total.

Starla and I pressed on together through everything. We did education for the staff in Tongi at the clinic as well as Bible studies and English classes where they were needed. She helped start a little clinic in Tilok, just outside the HOJ orphanage compound wall.

Life was slow in the village, but the days were definitely full. I would get up and see any sick kids from the orphanage before breakfast. Bengali village life chores dictated how daily life was conducted, including the laundry being done by hand in our pond. The pond was stocked with five kinds of fish and most of our vegetables were grown on the compound. We also grew our own rice. From the rice threshing pad to the pukur (our man-made pond), the kids learned the basics of Bangladeshi village life and how to live as Christians in their own land. We had fish out of the pond regularly. Once a week we had "meat day," where all the kids enjoyed chicken or goat curry. The day after was usually "half-meat day." I often cooked myself a Western meal on half-meat days, instead of having animal parts curry. After breakfast and prayer, it was off to school. Home of Joy had built a school for the village children as well as the home's orphans. I would routinely see any sick children from the school before going to start the clinic for the day. On an average day, I saw thirty to forty patients. One day, seventy patients came to the little mud hut outside the orphanage wall!

The Tilok clinic was organized as a tool to serve our neighbors. We wanted to provide for their needs also since the village was such a poor, underserved rural area. The clinic was purposefully set up opposite to Bangladeshi cultural norms. It was women and children first and men at the end—if time permitted. The men were not even allowed to wait at the clinic because the waiting porch was a social area where women could congregate, shed their burkas, and visit like neighbors.

My clinic was a mud and bamboo hut, just like their homes. For a window, I cut some slats out of the woven side of the building to let some light in. I pulled out more to let more light in, but even then my light was usually blocked by my audience at the window. There was no electricity or water. It was built to be a two-room establishment. However, one stormy night, a staff member's house blew down. He moved, family and all, into one side of my clinic—before it was even finished. So we just shared it. I shared the clinic with a chicken too, who laid an egg on my exam table nearly every day during the clinic hours; whichever patient was being seen at the time got to keep the egg.

The clinic became a blessing in so many ways. We saw fantastic answers to prayer and the Lord showed Himself regularly in marvelous ways. I charged the patients only 50 percent of the cost that I paid for medicines. Sometimes, I was paid in spinach, bananas, or eggs. Children being seen for malnutrition paid nothing and were fed as well. Malnutrition was a pervasive problem in our rural neighborhood. Those malnourished children were my special patients, and I expected to see them weekly. They were, of course, from the poorest families. I tried to teach them and usually gave prenatal care for the moms as well. The *Bangladesh Observer* newspaper reported thirty thousand children annually going blind from xerophthalmia, a vitamin A deficiency. Bangladeshis are as small as only generations of malnutrition can produce.

The clinic allowed me to get to know my neighbors pretty well. I would go on walks to visit them and then be able to share in their lives, sometimes even sharing the gospel—as was my primary purpose. On one wandering, someone came and presented me with a huge bunch of bananas right off the tree. I wondered what I would do with them all, as there weren't enough to give to all the kids, but too many to just eat. I was surprised that by the time I arrived back at the orphanage, I had actually consumed all sixteen little bananas.

One neighbor lady named Rohima (usually referred to as Mohammed's wife) came to the clinic with a badly infected wound on her thumb. I saw her many times and treated her with several courses of antibiotics. I performed an incision and drainage, but it was not improving. I suggested going to Khulna to have someone else do surgery. As a Muslim woman from a poor village family, this was not likely to happen. The value of girls and women left them little chance of needed help and sometimes survival. That was why the clinic was run the way it was.

Eventually, I made a bold move as a missionary nurse. I always prayed for my patients, right down the list, but usually just privately between just God and me. I told Rohima I'd like to pray for her. When she agreed I held her hand in mine and prayed out loud, in Bangla so she knew what I was saying and to whom I was praying. After she left, I didn't see her for days. That was unusual, because I had been changing her bandages daily. I was nervous that I had jumped in too soon with *Probhu Jishu* and made her upset or uncomfortable. When I saw her again, I asked how the hand was. She replied that since I had prayed, it was completely better. She proclaimed that the Lord had healed her. No longer swollen, draining, or hurting, she presented the hand. I felt ashamed of myself for the anxiety. Philippians 4:6 tells me clearly to "be anxious for nothing," but still I sometimes proceed with worry. I know God is faithful and trustworthy. He has proven it over and over again. This time, it helped to open doors with my dear Muslim neighbors.

Inroads had to be made separately among my Hindu neighbors, who comprised the other half of Tilok village. After Omar's new baby boy, Shettu, was born, a full day went by with no urine output. I was asked to intervene, but really nothing could be done out in the jungle. I explained that the most powerful tool in my kit for this was prayer. As I laid hands on him and prayed—in Bangla, in Jesus' name—an arc of urine shot up and sprinkled all over us as an instant and oh so obvious answer to prayer. After that, I was invited to pray often. When Shettu had his first rice-eating ceremony (*mukhi bhat*), I was invited to open in a prayer of thanks to Jesus and not Krishna. It was a joy, to be sure, as I saw God work. It was an honor to be used by Him and the thrill never lessened as time went by.

Opinions of me varied through the area. I overheard someone asking the *chowkidar* (gate guard) this question one day: "*Daktar Amma achay?*" (Is Dr. Mother here?) When I asked, I learned that was what I was called in the village around me. What an honor, as one of my own "heroes of the faith" was Amy Carmichael who was called Amma all her years of service in South India. To my face, people usually just called me "Sister." Sometimes, though, I heard mothers threaten their children to behave or I would give them an injection or something.

Murium was only two years old when she helped to set that straight for me. She was the daughter of a prominent Muslim man and his wife, Rohima, whose thumb I treated. They lived about a five-minute walk away from HOJ. Murium toddled all the way to the clinic alone, coming right in past the waiting people for an impromptu visit. Franticly, her mother came looking for her. Drowning in a pond was a distinct possibility for a toddler wandering alone in this neighborhood. Little Murium knew that coming to see me would be met with only hugs and smiles. The village children learned faster than the adults that I was not so scary—except maybe for the shots.

During all my time in Tilok, one of the highlights was walking around the village. As so many of the women had come to know my genuine care for them, I was invited into their lives at new levels. If I showed up walking past a yard, a child would often drag me closer, and then a coconut would appear as an invitation to sit. The day I sat under a mango tree with several women visiting together, I was realizing the dreams of so many years before—when I chose my minor in college to be cross-cultural ministry with an emphasis on ministry to Muslim women.

My year with Starla went by too fast. I would cry just thinking of her leaving, but the time approached regardless. We decided to have a little vacation before she left. She got to choose where. We went to Nepal for a couple of weeks for a well-deserved break. Our good friends with the Assembly of God church, Bob and Twyla McGurty, were traveling there with their family as well. Starla, who was still a lot stronger than I was, wanted to go trekking in the Himalayas. I agreed to do a "simple teahouse" trek. The guides made it sound like little old ladies would choose this option, but it was rugged hard. We went all the way to Annapurna base camp. We also went to a Tibetan refugee camp, riding around Nepal on motorcycles.

After a week of doing activities Starla had chosen, we did a few days of my choice: jungle hiking in the Royal Chitwan National Park to look for rhinos. This rhino experience has been another bond for us over the last twenty years. We hiked for miles looking for the elusive rhino through the Nepali national park. We adventured in dugouts and on elephant back, all the while seeing no rhinos. Eventually, after days, we gave up and were just chatting as we were going to see the Gharial Crocodile Farm. At that point, we finally saw a rhino … and it *charged* us. Our very young guide led it away, waving sticks in the air and running purposefully away from us. It was a terrifying, but exhilarating, moment—never to be forgotten. Starla had the camera up ready to shoot as I pulled her behind a tree away from the charging rhino. We decided at a distance was definitely the best way to get to see a rhino after all.

> Let my heart be broken with things that break
> the heart of God.
>
> —Bob Pierce, World Vision[5]

CHAPTER 8

A Broken Heart, 1993

the lord is near to the brokenhearted
and saves those who are crushed in
spirit
—psalm 34:18

I really missed Starla. After she left, I tried getting back to helping run the orphanage. I was also involved in two clinics, Bible studies, and other outreaches as best I could. After a couple of months, I realized part of my tired state of "hard to get up and go" was simply that I really didn't feel too well again. I went to rest at my friends' house in Dhaka, feeling feverish and flu-like. Sure enough, a viral febrile illness was causing my heart to beat way too fast. Slowly the fever resolved, but the very fast heart rate did not go away.

Little did I realize, but this would turn out to be another major watershed event in my life. I really had no idea at the time how drastically this event would impact my life. It's hard to explain how an experienced nurse, who can so readily recognize medical subtleties in clinic patients, can miss the altogether obvious symptoms when it becomes personal.

Despite having recently climbed in the Himalayas, my high heart rate made me suspect that I was out of shape and had better get some regular exercise. So I went to the American club to swim some laps. My heart rate then rose to well above two hundred beats per minute and would not slow down. I finally relented and decided to go to Dr. Wahab. He was a Bengali physician trained in Germany who treated many of the expatriates in the country. After lots of test and time, he diagnosed viral myocarditis.

His orders were bed rest for the week and return again the following week. A week of bed rest sounded pretty strict and inconvenient, but I moved to a friend's house—where there were no kids—to get some rest. Another missionary doctor friend, Dr. Helene, checked every day to see if my heart was tolerating the super fast 180–200 beats per minute nonstop.

At the next week's appointment with Dr. Wahab, after more tests, he told me to rest for another week and to see him again the next week. On the third consecutive week of being told "bed rest again," I finally asked, "How long might I expect this to continue?" His answer was an absolute shock to me. The plan was six to twelve months of complete bed rest.

Dr. Helene still came to the house every day. She asked me how my parents had responded to this news. I hadn't forced myself to call home yet, hesitating to call only to say that I was sick. My previous experiences with illness in Bangladesh had been such a worry for them. I wanted to delay calling until I started to at least improve. Dr. Helene, however, warned me that I could die here and now from this disease. I knew it would not be right for me to not even let them know I was sick. I needed to call home.

Before I even telephoned, God Himself had started to rally the troops, as He promised. "Before they call, I will answer;

while they are still speaking, I will hear" (Isaiah 65:24). When I talked to my mother, I tried to provide as much reassurance as I could muster. The conversation ensued without a breakdown. I assured her that I really didn't feel too awful, but I was profoundly exhausted. In fact, the fatigue was such that I would come to the dinner table and stare at the plate for ten minutes without moving. After those ten minutes passed, I would just give up and return to bed in tears. I didn't have the energy to eat anything.

My mom made a few frantic phone calls after she learned the diagnosis. When she called back the next day, the process of getting help had started to rapidly gain momentum. Mom did some research and determined that this was quite serious. One person she spoke to was Starla, who phoned Bangladesh after having arranged a doctor's appointment in Singapore. She was ready, if I needed her, to come to Bangladesh to escort me to the cardiologist in Singapore. Faith Willard also called saying she was suspicious that something was amiss. Her brother Peter in Maine, whom I had never met, had been burdened by God to pray and called to ask what she knew of my condition. Before I even began to let people in the United States know of my desperate situation, FOB supporters back in the States were praying for me in Bangladesh on the feeling that something was not right. Even an old boyfriend who supported me called Mom concerned that something was wrong with me. The Lord had alerted him and so many others that I needed prayer.

Considering all the factors, I concluded that if I had to get on a plane to Singapore to see a doctor, I might as well stay on that plane until it landed in Seattle. I had no connections or support in Singapore. The Lord orchestrated amazing help all along the journey. The hardest part, as always, was the Bangladesh leg. Life gets easier once that border is crossed. As a missionary, I lived with my visa in process; that means that government approval was always pending, and I lacked any permanent authorization to stay in the country. The process ensures that permission to stay can be denied at any time. My passport needed a visa stamped from the home department in Bangladesh in order to get out of Bangladesh. Usually, getting that stamp is a painfully slow process. Identifying the need for a medical evacuation accelerated the process considerably. The FOB national director took my doctor's note to the home department and returned with my stamped passport. Visa in hand, I arrived at the Bangladesh Biman office to book a flight out as soon as I could. When the airline person understood the problem, they required that a doctor accompany me. Also, I would have to pay for enough seats to be able to lie down the whole way and travel with oxygen. Adding a physician and these requirements made the cost staggering, way beyond the amount I carried for departure tickets. I told the clerk that was not financially possible. She asked me to leave and return without recounting any of the previous information. I complied, and returned right back to her desk. She knew the whole story and assisted getting me on a flight as quickly as possible.

Biman Bangladesh arranged for me to fly home, at twenty-five years old, as an unaccompanied minor. The flight attendants boarded me first and carried my bags. They assisted me from the airport in Bangkok and checked me into the hotel across the street where I had to stay for the night. God even provided another Bangladesh missionary family going home on leave to be on the plane with me. The McManus family had previously worked at Home of Joy, and they were glad to help me limp home.

I had not planned on going to the United States when I left the Home of Joy. I had simply gone to Dhaka for a rest with the intention of coming back strong and ready for duty. A FOB missionary offered to go to Khulna to pack up my things. Randa, who worked with the FOB widows' sewing project, volunteered to travel a whole day to the other end of the country to get what I needed. I tried to think of my necessities—and realized I really had none. My first concern was my mosquito net; then I recalled that we never used them back in Washington. I left with nothing but the carry-on bag I had brought to Dhaka. The only concern I had could be clearly seen thumping away wildly through my skinny chest. For three weeks, I had been unable to get up and do anything, even eat. I was beyond spent.

Nervous faces awaited me once again at SeaTac airport. This was my third very dramatic homecoming. Mom, Dad, and Starla were so relieved to see me drag through customs. Instead of the usual runabout and visiting, my parents took me straight to a hotel so I could get into bed. My friends were alerted to where I was so they could come and visit me there. Everyone wished they could do something to make it all better. Dad asked if he could get me anything. When I requested an apple, he walked to the grocery store instead of driving so he could put more personal effort into it.

After a couple of days on planes and, indeed, a couple of years in Bangladesh, I really wanted a hot shower. Mom offered to help me. I stubbornly refused, reminding her that I was twenty-five years old and insisting I was capable of showering on my own. I stepped into the shower and promptly collapsed to the floor. Mom came in responding with worry cloaked between near tears and anger. *Now* could she help?

For the next four months, I was mostly confined to either my bed at home or a bed in my parent's van. I went to the Spokane

Heart Institute frequently. Otherwise, people came to see me. I ventured to church on occasion. People wanted to see me, and those were the folks to whom I needed to prove that I was still alive. I remember lying on the pew at Northview Bible Church with my heart racing away uncontrollably. Things looked and sounded grim, but it was really a time of blessed intimacy with God. I was forced to spend time with Him alone like never before.

I was only twenty-five years old, yet I was not shocked by the prospect of dying that young. I told my family that I was either going to die from this disease or I was going to return to Bangladesh. For the first time since I was twelve years old, they genuinely hoped that I would make it to Bangladesh. Most of the time, I felt a real peace despite not knowing the eventual outcome. I tried my best to be content in my circumstances, like Paul (Philippians 4:11). I made every effort to rejoice always and pray unceasingly (1 Thessalonians 5:16–17). And I dreamed of Bangladesh, my other homeland.

> Perhaps you shall see the Sundarban bird whirling
> in the evening breeze
> or you may hear an owl calling from the branch
> of the silk cotton tree.
> Perhaps a child shall fling a fist of paddy on the
> grass of your courtyard
> or a boy shall sail a boat with torn white sail down
> the muddy waters of the Rupsha River.
> Amidst all this you shall find me in Bangladesh.
> —Jibanananda Das

During all that time, only once for about ten minutes, did I break down and sob. I lay on the couch at Starla's house with her and cried tears of fear and sadness.

Starla drove me all the way to Michigan to visit Dr. Dave and Nan Walter, our close friends from language school in Bangladesh. They were just home for a short stay for the birth of their new baby girl, Grace. They were very surprised to see me at all, but especially looking bluish, skinny, and short of breath. I'm certain they did not expect to see me back in Bangladesh again. It wasn't until years later that they communicated how they felt about that visit together. "Worry" was rather an understatement.

I read nearly the entire Bible during those months. Though it was wearisome to have to stay in bed for so long, God made it a blessed time of intimate fellowship like few have the chance to experience. I had almost no responsibilities or obligations. God blessed this time and made it an unusually, unexpectedly rich. Bill—the former boyfriend who had been alerted by the Lord to my situation—came to my parents' house often to visit, as did other friends. People would be beside me when I would wake up, just to play games or watch NBA basketball. I spent so much time having to just lay in bed during the NBA finals in 1993 that I developed quite an interest in the game. I consumed books, played board games, and napped the weeks away while my swollen heart pounded madly.

I set a goal that if I could get medical clearance to get out of bed by the last week of camp at Sweyolakan, I would volunteer as their nurse for a week. I had gone to this Camp Fire camp in Idaho for many stays during childhood, so it was something to aim for. In late August, I began being able to get about and started working toward rebuilding some long lost strength and endurance. Having been sick with myocarditis since February and sick in January with the precipitating viral illness, I did not have much endurance or strength. But I made my goal of going for a week to Sweyolakan. Not a lot was required of me there, and it was healing to body and spirit to slowly amble about in the sunshine at Lake Coeur d'Alene.

One day an emergent call came on the radio for the nurse. I was needed way up on a hill where the campers had gone for a lunch hike. A camper with bee allergies had been stung and was reacting. I needed to give her an epinephrine shot immediately—and it was a long ways away. The camp speedboat delivered me to the area near where they had hiked. I transferred into a smaller fishing boat that took me to a rock wall; the campers were up at the top. I wondered how I was going to manage this. As I started to scale the wall, first aid kit in hand, a Scripture verse came to mind. In my heart, I heard, "With my God, I can scale a wall" (2 Samuel 22:30). I didn't know I even knew that verse, but having read the Scripture my whole life, it was at the ready when I needed it. God spoke to me and enabled me to do what seemed impossible. God's Word really does not return empty. The little girl who had been stung was fine too.

For nearly my whole life, I have prayed for God to break my heart with things that break His. I truly wanted to be that connected to the heart of God. The prayer was written by World Vision's founder, Bob Pierce. "Let my heart be broken with things that break the heart of God." I had been living that for years, and it seemed that God had answered those prayers again and again. I had many people who loved me, begging me to save some heart for myself as well. I heard often, "Bangladesh really did break your heart, Jill."

As blessed as the time of fellowship with God was, the overall experience of six months of bed rest was absolute drudgery. I decided that if I was ever told again I had the option of six long months of bed rest or death, I was going to choose death. I couldn't wait to get moving again.

Many people were moved to pray for me, a debt I can never fully repay. Just as when people prayed for me when they thought my life was in danger during the flood, I really wanted those prayers to be targeted for the nation of Bangladesh. I brought home a very large bag of Bangladeshi coins, *poisha*. I gave out these coins often in a reverse offering scenario: pass the plate, and take some coins. I asked people to put them where they would be seen and found frequently. I explained that when the poisha showed up, they were to pray for the nation of Bangladesh and the hearts of people there. I have some still in my purse, wallet, pockets, etc. I pray for Bangladesh now as much as I did back when I was twelve years old. Except now, many of the *National Geographic* faces have names and histories. I still picture throngs of Bengalis worshipping around the throne of Christ, but each of them is a loved individual that Christ knows personally.

> Circumstances may appear to wreck our lives and God's plans, but God is not helpless among the ruins.
>
> —Eric Liddell[6]

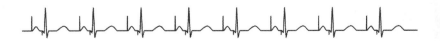

CHAPTER 9

A Miraculous Return

here am i; send me.
—isaiah 6:8 nasb

After my intensely spiritual near-death experience, I was more motivated than ever to share about my amazing God. It was a reward like never before to get to go back to Bangladesh in October 1993. I surmised that having lived through myocarditis, *nothing* could stop me now. I was meant to be a missionary nurse in Bangladesh. It was so thoroughly and deeply the desire of my heart.

Having earlier informed my parents that I was either going to die or return to Bangladesh, my mother had made the decision to accompany me to see and experience firsthand what drew me there. Mom wanted to see what I had been up to during these years. She refers to it still as her "*National Geographic* experience." More than ever before, she was grateful for her gray hair, as the Asian respect for elders made her more comfortable. Each member of my family is quite tall, and my mom recalls that she felt like Goliath from the time she set foot in Asia. On our way through Thailand and in Bangladesh, she was intrigued and shocked by noises that were new to her. At the guesthouse in Thailand, mom asked about the loud whooping noise. That was made by the monkeys in the tree, which were much more frequently heard than seen. The trees are so thick that the monkeys hide well among them. *Tor-tangs* and *tik-tikis*, types of lizards that would scurry along on the walls, scared her. When one got stuck and died in the door hinge in a room at the orphanage, I told her I would get it out of there. She said, "No. Leave it there as a warning to any others." When we first arrived at the orphanage, I announced we were having chicken for dinner. She was not accustomed to such a primitive level of life and hadn't noticed the live chickens on the porch that would soon be dinner.

My mother was overwhelmed by what had become rather ordinary to me over time. Before her trip, she had been so worried about things she heard in the news. Instead of feeling great relief from seeing how I was living, she gained many more concerns in areas she hadn't even considered before. She learned to worry if mine was the last car on the ferry and at risk of falling into the crocodile-infested waters of the Rupsha River. Now she would also wonder if there was electricity to make the fan work and if I would be able to get a baby taxi on a busy day. As a total package experience though, Mom came to better understand what my love for Bangladesh was all about.

Looking past the filth and poverty, there is considerable beauty and much to be appreciated in Bangladesh. A line in the national anthem, *Amar Sonar Bangla* (*My Golden Bengal*), reads "the smell of your mangoes makes me crazy." I loved the tropical abundance available, especially lychees. For the short season of this fruit, I would eat them to the exclusion of all other foods. As I introduced Mom to my regional favorites, she appreciated the amazingly lush fauna. It is the lovely people, however, who endeared Bangladesh to her so much.

John Sajjon, "Boby"—who had been the HOJ music teacher—had become the Home of Joy school headmaster. He was no longer an occasional guest. Instead, he spent long hours at the orphanage and new school. He was "a man after God's own heart" and very active in the kingdom work of Bangladesh. We worked together on many projects. He and the orphanage director, Aroti Howlader, did not always get along well, but he tried to be respectful. By his life, he taught the boys at HOJ about growing up as godly men. His amazing music always served as a soothing balm to my soul. I would treat his sicknesses and teach English classes with him and was rewarded with tabla music nearly anytime I requested.

Going to the Home of Joy was the highlight for my mom. It was certainly my favorite place in the country. There she met Kristine, her namesake, whom she was financially supporting. Mom seriously prayed that she would not get lice, but she opted to hold the kids despite the risk. The only times Mom wasn't at my side was when she would garner the courage to go to the children's building on her own. She couldn't communicate at all without me, but the mashis were friendly and all the children were inquisitive and loved to be cuddled. While all the staring outside the orphanage made her uncomfortable, inside she didn't mind people getting close enough to touch her and ask questions she couldn't understand.

We were able to enjoy a birthday outing during her visit there. I used to take the kids out for their birthday once a month. Most of the children did not know their actual date of birth, so we assigned them a date to recognize their birthday.

Every Friday night at the orphanage, we had an evening talent show for family entertainment. Many of the kids were trained in cultural dance. For those of us there for every Friday performance, it was fairly predictable. Mom really enjoyed seeing the littlest girls dressed up and performing traditional Bengali dancing. The Bengalis seem to have the tradition in their genetics. She enjoyed more of the food that she thought she would, especially for a person who hates all fish. Though she was only there for a couple of weeks, she got a taste for how life goes and a glimpse of the countryside. Mom was enriched and blessed through her trip to Bangladesh.

When I returned to the Home of Joy, I was about nine months behind in my work and had a *lot* to do. I had new priorities too. Those goals were simply rest, exercise, shower, and read the Bible every day. Basic essentials really, but it was an exceptional day when I could accomplish all that and my work responsibilities too. There was no Starla to help me or take care of me. I took more regular breaks, especially going down to Malumghat to visit the Walters. They called me their favorite but most boring guest. I would eat nonstop and sleep long hours on every visit. I would sometimes fly to Cox's Bazaar, and I had a chance to see Bangladesh's beautiful white sand beaches. God brought other people into my life to bless me and make my world more pleasant and manageable. I recognize each of these people as direct answers to prayer and provision from the hand of God. God knows just how to bless me. My favorite blessings from the Lord are always those wrapped so beautifully in human skin, just as He was.

Two young men who had just graduated from premed Ivy League schools had come to Bangladesh to investigate the option of long-term missions. They helped both at the clinic and the orphanage as well as generally kept life light for almost six months. Mark Saadeh and Adam Barton met when they came to Bangladesh and became fast friends. The three of us enjoyed our time together a great deal. We did some Friday night performances for the kids during the weekly show. In the spirit of the Proclaimers music group from Scotland, we called it the Poverty and Failure tour. We didn't call it that when we sang at church for Easter. If laughter is the best medicine, Mark and Adam helped keep me much healthier. They fueled my basketball interest as well. During the March Madness NCAA tournament, Adam's brother sent a fax daily to give updates. We would venture to the city of Khulna to learn how things were in the basketball world via the World Relief office fax machine. We spent many evenings on the roof playing the "Up and Down the River" card game like fiends. They learned Bangla well enough to manage without translator assistance, which was very helpful.

One day, they helped to spearhead the attack on lice at HOJ. The older girls were informed if they didn't help each other get rid of the lice, there would be a massive head shaving event to remedy the problem. Adam and Mark were the first to initiate things and get shaved to the skin. Then we used razors and clippers and made nearly every head at HOJ bald. While long hair for Bangladeshi women is important, young children generally get their heads shaved every year because it is believed doing that makes their hair grow back thicker and darker. There was laughter and music while we shaved away. We burned all the hair, and the lice were definitively conquered.

Not many people are immunized against vaccine-preventable diseases in Bangladesh. Mark and Adam were there during a few months of absolute epidemic at HOJ and the surrounding village. It was four months of continuous infectious diseases. Sohel, an eight-year-old boy at the orphanage, was the first to come to me with a fever and not feeling well. I had him rest but did not isolate him. The next day, a rash appeared unlike I had ever seen before. Measles* hardly ever occurs in America, because we are an immunized nation. In fact, because it is so contagious, a single case is flagged as an outbreak. By the time I determined the origin of the rash, the epidemic was already underway. Over the next few months, I managed forty-seven cases of measles and simultaneously forty-four cases of mumps.* I was even more grateful for Mark and Adam then, because it was a nearly impossible task. Stephen, one of the orphanage babies, became desperately ill when he contracted the mumps. After he survived, there seemed to be lasting cerebral palsy–type problems. Joseph, about six years old, got an encephalitis* complication and had trouble with school from then on. I maintained a separate room at the orphanage, keeping five to ten sick kids quarantined at a time while caring for them.

The epidemics also surged through the HOJ school and the surrounding village community. I was desperate for some vaccines to prevent further outbreaks. A contact at the World Health Organization provided me with coolers full of vaccines. All I had to do was return the coolers with numbers of how many were vaccinated when we were finished. Mark and Adam were eager to learn how to give the injections, and I was more than happy to spread the workload. As the children were so fond of the fun uncles, many rushed to them to get injections—until they noticed the difference in my techniques. They were able to notice the considerable increase in finesse that comes with experience.

Seeing Patients at the Clinic

Vaccines come to the forefront of my mind when I think of Bangladesh. Every trip into the country was a calculated risk of infections. When visitors were planning on coming, I would recommend a list of shots to receive before their arrival. Though I had been fully vaccinated for typhoid three times, I still acquired the disease twice. The International Center for Cholera Research is located in Dhaka for a good reason. The measles and mumps inoculations were obviously effective, because no immunized people contracted the disease during the outbreak.

Another big outbreak problem occurred shortly after that one had resolved. This was a bona fide bubonic plague outbreak, epicentered in Surat, India. There was a panic of antibiotics being hoarded, even in Bangladesh. I was relieved that I had gone out of my way to receive the whole bubonic plague vaccine series in the States, though it was a real hassle at the time.

The border between India and Bangladesh was sealed for a bit. When planes from India were allowed to land, men with chemical suits boarded the planes first before people could disembark. They sprayed chemicals on the passengers before allowing them off the plane into Bangladesh. If you are at all surprised that they can do that, understand that this is also in a country where they drive a truck through town and spray DDT to help abate the malaria problem. The malarial risk more than justifies the risk associated with chemical spraying. Using mosquito sprays, coils, and nets over bedding helps, but those measures do not stop all the malaria. When I first arrived, I took malaria pills every Monday faithfully. Every Monday was then filled with nausea and stomach cramping followed by vomiting and diarrhea. Eventually I stopped taking the pills, risking the threat of malaria as opposed to the promise of weekly feeling miserable.

Aside from the germs, lice, scabies, and mosquitos, there were bigger "bugs," and even animals, to contend with. I used to joke when I heard a noise that the cockroaches were moving furniture in my room. Appreciating the story of *Rikki Tikki Tavi*, I loved that there were mongooses dashing in the yard at times—until one day when we discovered a king cobra in the children's building. I had never feared snakes at all until that day. This one hid up a drainpipe once it was cornered. Knowing such a deadly snake was present, it could not be ignored. With a ready army of men (and me) to fight it, we lit a fire at the drainpipe entrance to force it out. It shot out of the drain pipe and came up with the hood flared and striking in any direction it could. We humans rained down blows repeatedly on it. Adrenaline surged in a strike or be struck situation. I found myself more nervous about the snakes and mongooses—and had the lawn trimmed right down to the dirt.

Sometimes it was not far from our mind that tigers were in the nearby jungle, but we never had any problems with them.

Near Malumghat, though, the same could not be said of rogue elephants.

The wild creatures were nothing compared to Mother Nature's rule in Bangladesh. The summer months are unbelievably sticky and relentlessly hot. Floods are an annually expected season of the year. The whole nation is a giant flood plain, and the storms are impressive by any standards. One day it was raining sideways through the open windows in the hallway at the orphanage. Adam decided he needed to check to be sure some windows were closed. When he came running back to the other building, something struck him. He came in holding his head, laughing that he thought he'd been hit with a coconut. Mark and I assured him that he would be dead on the lawn if a coconut had hit him. Even a leaf at wind speeds like that can be painful. It was blowing so hard that when Aroti, the orphanage director returned, she was very shaken. She had been driving, and the wind had blown the van right over on its side. The sheet metal roof on the garage had lifted off and cut straight through the power lines. I was there for a few of Bangladesh's famous cyclones as well.

Besides the nursing and physical care, people's spiritual lives were of utmost concern to me. I conducted a spiritual inventory with every child at the orphanage. I prayed with each individually and searched what was on their hearts. I made an effort to personalize God so they could come to understand Him at their own level. Four children made first-time commitments to the Lord. In all my years of ministry, or in anything else I have ever done, nothing surpasses praying with people to enter the family of Christ. Every time is the best ever, no matter how many times I've been privileged to be present for the miracle.

The mission risked getting into trouble with the government for people "becoming Christians." I could deny converting people in all honesty and sincerity, as I am incapable of making anyone a Christian. That is expressly a work of God that no man can accomplish. I've saved lives, as a nurse and as a lifeguard. I've delivered babies and given birth myself. Many things in life are great, but being a part of the transition from spiritual death to life will always be the best thing in the world. Pioneer missionary C. T. Studd said, "I cannot tell you what joy it gave me to bring the first soul to Jesus Christ. I have tasted almost all the pleasures that this world can give. I do not suppose there is one I have not experienced, but I can tell you that those pleasures were as nothing compared to the joy that the saving of one soul gave me."[7]

I've been to several Billy Graham crusades. As soon as the intro rolls for *Just As I Am*, tears of joy are running down my face. I prayed for years that God would give me His heart for His people. The joy I experience when people call on God and the pain of seeing separation from Him lets me know that prayer has been one well answered.

The spiritual lives of my patients and neighbors were my primary concern. The longer I was in the country, the more I was able to share my motivation for staying in Bangladesh. Returning to Bangladesh after having myocarditis spoke volumes to many people there. They understood that I had been sick almost to death. I worked hard to come back, despite the risk for myself, out of a love for them all.

A young Muslim neighbor girl came to be a fixture at the clinic. Confidentiality is not at all an expectation there, and she would sit near me and listen to everything I said. She would come to just be with me anytime she could. Though she was only fifteen, Mukta had already been married and divorced. She saw no hope for her future. It was a daily pleasure to share about the

One who loved her and would never leave and forsake her, like she had been forsaken.

Mukta was there to witness when a couple of patients gave up the amulets⋆ they wore for protection, to try protection from God instead. A lady came holding the talisman around her neck saying, *"Kono shokti noi"* (This has *no* power). What a breakthrough to be able to explain that she really could not expect much power or protection from this inanimate piece of metal. I carry a couple of those abandoned amulets on my keychain still as trophies of hearts won to Christ.

SPU SPRINT had connected with me while I was in the United States. For the first time ever, there was a SPRINT Bangladesh team. They came over Christmas break from school instead of when it is miserably hot in the summer. This gave me company and a chance to share my passion for Bangladesh and all the people there. As is often the case, God gave me one person who especially touched my heart. Elizabeth Thorndike had grown up on the mission field herself in Morocco and was now studying nursing and missions at SPU to become a missionary herself. It did my heart good to have someone so like me to connect with. Encouraging her was a reminder to myself of why I was doing what I was doing. The team all reveled in the children and had a unique Christmas, I am sure. Christmas in Bangladesh is whatever you make it. I focused on Jesus in my half-Hindu, half-Muslim neighborhood. While I was legally limited in what I could say while sharing my faith, the visitors were not. They were just visiting. I shepherded them in Christmas caroling in the village. We would sing Bangla and English songs, and then I would "translate" to tell them what the team had come to share. It afforded me such a great opportunity to speak into my neighbor's lives.

There were challenges having eight more bideshis (foreigners) to translate for and to watch over. From their arrival at Zia airport, trying to keep them together and away from where they shouldn't be had its moments. We stayed at the Southern Baptist guesthouse in Dhaka before traveling south to Khulna. By the time we reached the guesthouse, one girl, Debbie, no longer had her suitcase of clothes.

When I took them shopping, we had to use several rickshaws. After losing some of them on our first trip out and having to search for miles for quite some scary time, I learned to control the travel situation better. I would collect as many transports as necessary, give directions to all the drivers together, and then haggle a fair price. If they would stay together all the way, the fare was increased considerably. Bringing the team back to Dhaka, I had trouble finding enough vehicles to hire in Dhaka's old city. We had taken the twenty-four-hour *Rocket* ship upriver from Khulna to get back to Dhaka. Though the boat is called the *Rocket*, it is the slowest way to travel—but also worth the lovely overnight trip. I managed to hire a transport truck, for a lot of taka, to take twelve of us and a mountain of luggage to the guesthouse. That driver got lots of crazy stares driving ten giggling foreigners and a couple of local people around in the back of a giant, well-decorated cargo truck. Upon delivery at the Baptist guesthouse, the truck driver had to wait for a dozen cameras to commemorate the journey.

SPU SPRINT-Bangladesh made it a great Christmas in 1993, having brought a whole Christmas celebration package with them. During their time at the orphanage, they made shirts with all the kids. They brought gifts as well and did all the wrapping for me. I got some help to make the Christmas tree and art projects to decorate the orphanage.

On the holiday where we celebrate the birth of our infant king, we got a special gift at HOJ. A visiting ophthalmologist from England was working in Khulna. He'd had a baby girl abandoned at their project. He and his wife brought Esther out to HOJ, so we got a new baby, too, for our holiday festivities.

There were some holiday traditions that I was glad to leave behind, ie not being a fan of fruitcake. The British couple who came to celebrate Christmas with us brought both baby Esther and a fruitcake. Despite being half a world away, I still had to politely partake of another fruitcake.

In Bengali, Christmas is called *Boro Din*, or Big Day. We sang *Happy Big Day* and celebrated so the whole non-Christian community surrounding us could understand that we really had something to celebrate.

As part of the activities for the team, we took a boat excursion into the *SundarBan* Forest. Tilok village is near the outskirts of the famed enormous mangrove forest that defines the delta geography of the region. We ventured in with armed Forest Service guides to protect us from the beloved—and feared—Royal Bengal tiger. Though I had lived close to the SundarBans for a long time, it was a great opportunity to take such a grand outing to this underwater forest. We rented a big boat and looked for animals and experienced terrain that is so unlike any other place. The topography was like another planet, with the spikes of roots coming up from the ground for air.

We occasionally tried to plan special outings for the children and staff at the orphanage, but it was laborious. It was unwieldy to travel with such a large number of people, many of whom really did not travel well. The first time we did a HOJ picnic, there were eighty-two of us on the bus we rented. For the long fifty miles to Jessore, all the kids were vomiting. We stopped at a roadside shop and bought plastic bags. I medicated all the kids at the picnic site. Everyone had a terrific time, but they slept all the way home in a Dramamine-induced stupor. Puke-covered Ishmael, one of Bombay boys, lay asleep on my lap the whole way home. We did picnics annually after that, but we stayed much closer to home.

A wedding was always a grand reason for a celebration. If there was any Home of Joy connection, we would take as many children with us as we could manage. We traveled to a remote village with thirty-two people in our little van once. Bengali weddings are a cultural, social experience like few others. Hindu, Muslim, and Christian weddings are all entirely different procedures. This Hindu wedding was made up of three days of festivities. Many Bengali weddings have the common element of a sobbing young girl being taken away from her family. Often she lives as a slave to all in her husband's family home, at least until her first child is born. Arranged marriages are still the norm, and the bride and groom often do not know each other at all.

Faith and I went on a few dramatic excursions by ourselves. There had been a lot of love, prayer, and concern invested in those seventeen boys rescued from Bombay. Most of them had been returned to their families while I was home sick with myocarditis. We went to find them in the villages, check on them, and give them a gift of the Injil Sharif* (the New Testament in Muslim Bengali language). The older Carey Bible uses a different vocabulary unfamiliar to the Muslim population, though many Muslim background people have and still do come to Christ through the Carey Bible. We traveled deep into villages where some had never seen a white face before. Once the boys felt assured that we were not there to reclaim them, they were quite happy to see Faith and me. All the boys could speak proper Bangla by this time. Whether they had been kidnapped or sold by their desperately needy families was never verified. We felt relieved to see them looking fed and content with the families we had returned them to. Those families knew that we were Christians and that we cared deeply for their children. Sometimes, seeds have to be planted without any knowledge of what the Lord will do from there.

The orphanage continued to thrive with new additions of both children and programs. A new school outside the HOJ wall had been constructed—the Home of Joy High School—for the Tilok village children to attend. The clinic was well established.

Mukti, another little handicapped cherub, had been brought to the orphanage. She was always smiling, but she was making very little developmental progress. Trying to teach her to walk was a real challenge. She was too afraid to let go. I concocted an amusing trick to have her grip be transferred to her own shirt. She would toddle about holding the shoulders and neckline of her own shirt, desperately "holding herself up."

I was connecting with people, from the mayor to the farmers throughout the upazila,★ and able to blend into the workforce to get all kinds of work done. I was also able to share the love of the Lord with the people He gave me to love.

Rita—my star pupil from my International Needs days— found me back in Bangladesh, connected to Home of Joy. She was too old for the orphanage by this point and was in the same unspeakable poverty as are many in Bangladesh. Rita resided with her new husband in the toxic filth of a slum behind the cholera hospital. Knowing what she had been taught, I was able to hire her to come on staff at Home of Joy. It was such a joy to get reconnected and have the opportunity to get her and her family back on their feet again.

Hazel St. John, a friend of Faiths', came to visit from England a couple of times. Hazel had been a missionary in Lebanon for nearly forty years. Her sister, Patricia St. John, wrote many challenging stories such as *Star of Light* during her missionary years in Morocco. When Hazel visited us, she retold some of Patricia's stories at our evening devotion time in the orphanage. It was my privilege to translate the stories into Bangla. The children were blessed by the stories of God's working. I was equally blessed to be close to such magnificent examples of godliness in the lives of Hazel and Patricia.

The ministry was thriving, but trouble was always present as well. The nature of Bangladesh government allows for considerable unrest. Martial law had been declared eighteen times in the first twenty-five years of nationhood. Often a change of government was done by a hostile takeover. Despite being called a republic, at that time Bangladesh had yet to experience a peaceful election process. During the 1994 election period, violence escalated dangerously. Political strikes, called *hartals*, were prevalent. They were scheduled and organized by specific political parties and enforced emphatically. The penalties for not following the hartals could be getting bricked, burned, beat up, etc.

At one point, I had decided I'd had enough hartals. They were really getting in the way of productivity. So I decided I was through with honoring the hartals. I paid exorbitantly to be taken out of the village while the mandate rang out from the mosque to stop the NGOs. *"NGO ar cholbay na"* (The NGO will not go on anymore). The rickshaw driver was glad to have an opportunity to make money for himself, and I needed to get to Khulna to speak to the mayor about this.

As I approached the ferryghat, I disembarked from the rickshaw to walk the rest of the way to avoid causing trouble for the driver. God flexed again that day when I needed a miracle. Though I created the need for the miracle, I have found that God faithfully watches over His idiots. I have been grateful many times for that. An angry mob of hundreds of men with sticks and stones were at the ferryghat to enforce the hartal. They rushed the rickshaw and slashed his tires for being out, but the penalty was not more severe because he did not have a passenger. That was the miracle. At the same ferryghat where I was normally stared at by literally hundreds of people, I walked through the angry crowd to the river's edge with nobody even turning their head to look at me. I was somehow completely cloaked by God. I have no idea if they saw nothing, or maybe a cow, or what? None of those sticks, meant for stopping the NGOs, pointed toward me or threatened me.

I asked a *nowkha-wallah* (boatman) if he could take me across the river for a generous wage, but the mob had taken their paddles until the end of the hartal. I quietly slipped into an empty yard and sat for the remaining hours of the hartal before I could get to town to get the necessary work done. It was honestly another one of those days when I should have been killed; instead, I saw the Lord move mountains—again. My spiritual boldness grew more as I saw God's power. I knew increasingly that "from everyone who has been given much, much would be demanded" (Luke 12:48).

During Christmas break 1994, another SPU team came. Because of the political instability, I needed to get them out of the country. The scheduled hartal was potentially going to cause serious bloodshed, and it was my responsibility to keep them safe. I took them to Kolkata to sidestep the political upheaval. They were thrilled at the unexpected opportunity. We traveled overland through the Benapole border crossing and took the train into Kolkata at Sealdah station. My first trip to Kolkata in

1988—during my SPRINT team mission—was unnerving. I had returned a few times, and surprisingly I really enjoyed the urban Indian enclave by this time. My first time into Bangladesh, a missionary was excited about her upcoming vacation to Kolkata; I was mortified at the thought. It was easy to appreciate it more later.

Kolkata, the capital of West Bengal, is the center for Bengali speakers. I could get around Kolkata because I knew the Bengali spoken in Bangladesh. Many strange foreigners visit India; that meant I was not intriguing at all to the masses. I could go out and be left alone, sometimes even ignored.

Oddly, my favorite place to visit when I was away from HOJ in Kolkata was Mother Teresa's orphanage, Shishu Bhavan. It was just a short walk from where I usually stayed in the city. I really loved caring for Bengali babies at HOJ, but when I was in Shishu Bhavan I could simply hold and love the babies; nobody would come to bring me any of the problems at all. That was a respite enough.

Going to Mother Teresa's was a significant event for me that trip. One of the girls on the team begged to go meet Mother Teresa. I am not inclined to go meet someone famous just to chase after them. I promised to take the team only to her projects. If she happened to be visiting there, we would meet her. I made this comment in front of an Indian friend I had taken them to meet. Vijayan announced that Mother Teresa had specific hours when she would greet people at the Mother House. At that point, I was fairly obligated to take them.

The team was excited to meet Mother Teresa. Some were giddy with the anticipation. Personally, it was a more profound moment than I had expected. She asked each one where he or she came from and spoke for a moment. When she asked me, I replied that Khulna, Bangladesh, was home. She said, "Oh, you're a coworker." Meeting this humble woman of faith blessed my heart. We shared our stories in our adopted tongue. The language in her heart, too, was Bangla.

When the violent hartal ended, I escorted the SPRINT team safely back to Khulna. They delivered Christmas to the orphans again, bearing gifts, games, candies, and decorations. They also provided a grand feast for the neighboring Christian community as well. Joipur colony, near Tilok village, was home to a very small, poor Christian fellowship. We joined them for worship on Christmas Day. Often I didn't attend the local Christian services, because my presence was a distraction for them. Sure enough, at Joipur, they asked if I could share a word from the Lord with them. God gave them a gift, which blessed me a great deal as well. Though I hadn't prepared a sermon, God had a message for His people in the colony. I was so honored to be the mouthpiece to deliver that message of love. Boro Din 1994 was fragrant with the aroma of Christ as we worshipped together the God who came as a baby and became Father to us all. The believers joined us later that night at the orphanage, en masse, to continue celebrating together. We danced all night long on the rice threshing pad singing, "This is the Big Day, brother. God has come."

It is always exciting to be used by God, but honestly it is sometimes alarming. One day, our driver—who lived in the other side of my clinic building—came to me worried about his sick little girl. I went to examine Lipika immediately but found nothing too disconcerting. I rechecked a few hours later, as promised, to see if she had improved and was taken aback. She was not able to open her mouth at all. It was painfully clenched. When I had seen her earlier, there was nothing that made me suspect tetanus.★ I had a check in my spirit upon assessing her again, a nudge from the Holy Spirit as I puzzled at the medical picture.

The Lord alerted me with that gentle prodding, so I knew it was not a medical problem at all but rather a case of demon possession.

This was an arena I had read about but was not practiced in. I gathered a couple of strong Christian workers with me for the fight to come. Mrs. Biswas, who lived at HOJ as the grandmother, was a Bible woman herself. She joined me as we prayed with power, endurance, and faith for a two-hour battle. Whenever we uttered the name of the Lord, little Lipika growled like an animal. She writhed, but she still could not open her jaws. When she finally could, her mouth opened and she screamed loud and long before collapsing with sobs. It was a hard-fought victory like I had not experienced before, but it was not surprising in a land where so many demons are worshipped. I worshipped in amazement at seeing God's hand again. I whispered another prayer at the conclusion. "Thank you, God, but let's never do that again, if that's alright with You."

After it happened the first time, though, there was once again the need to cast out demons. I put both feet and one arm in the work. With the other arm, I held the hand of Jesus like a death grip. Many of the things I did—clinics, education, and general problem solving—were challenging, but there was a verse to define this struggle. It was a work only of the Lord. "This kind can only come out by prayer" (Mark 9:29).

Besides political and spiritual disturbances, there was some social turmoil to work through as well. Our night guard, Faruq, was discovered to be the reason for some theft at the compound. He was not actually stealing, but he was accepting *baksheesh*★ from the neighbors to be "asleep" and allow theft to happen undisturbed in the night. After investigation revealed the answer to the disappearing water pump and more, Faruq was appropriately discharged from our service. His response was to go to the authorities and press charges against us for firing him on religious grounds. Christians are a persecuted minority in Bangladesh, so for a Muslim to say we fired him on those grounds stirs up trouble. It would be overturned in court, but it could cause trouble along the way. As far as I know, the charges still stand, but nothing really ever came of it. We did get the pump back, too, during the investigation process.

Social structure and politics clashing caused trouble throughout Bangladesh and the region. Just as the Christians are not usually fairly represented, neither are the groups of tribal people living throughout the country. The Chittagong Hill Tracts are home to many of those tribes. They are Bangladeshi nationals, but are not Bengali. They consider themselves from a tribe, not from a political country with its well-defined borders. Throughout South and Southeast Asia, the tribal people are often landless and without rights. As Bangladesh struggled with overcrowding, people would go to live in the Hill Tracts where land was "available." The *Shanti Bahini* (peace force militia) continuously maintained an armed military force in the area as the dispute grew.

The tribal section of the Bangladesh border is shared with North East India, which has similar political struggles. Also, during the 1990s, more people came to the Hill Tracts out of the political turmoil in neighboring Burma. The Rohingya Muslim group was being chased, indeed by ethnic cleansing, out of their country. Several UNHCR (United Nations High Commission for Refugees) refugee camps were established in the Hill Tracts along the border. Anyone who runs *into* Bangladesh as a refugee truly has no place to go.

New people were unwelcome in the overcrowded camps. That added to the tension in an already unstable area. Bangladesh could not afford to provide basic needs for the hundreds of thousands of people escaping the treachery next door. The BDR (Bangladesh Rifles), the border patrol guards, were busy. The whole nation did not seem to know what to do with the situation, just as it had been with the Biharis before. Bangladesh was meant to be a sanctuary for Muslims, which both the Rohingyas and Biharis are, but also a land for the Bengalis specifically. Many problems remain today, especially as the disaster in Burma continues and changes daily.

> Life is pitiful, death so familiar, suffering and pain so common, yet I would not be anywhere else. Do not wish me out of this or in any way seek to get me out, for I will not be got out while this trial is on. These are my people, God has given them to me, and I will live or die with them for Him and His glory.
>
> —Gladys Aylward (missionary to China)[8]

CHAPTER 10

A Life-Changing Decision, 1995

but if any of you lacks wisdom, let him
ask of god, who gives to all generously
and without reproach, and it will be given
to him.

—James 1:5 nasb

do not be anxious about anything, but in
every situation, by prayer and petition,
with thanksgiving, present your
requests to god. and the peace of god,
which transcends all understanding,
will guard your hearts and your minds
in christ jesus.

—Philippians 4:6-7

As with during my time at Savar years before, just being in love
with Bangladesh did not exempt me from being affected by the
struggles of the nation. The political unrest, the spiritual darkness,
and the constant health battles easily made me homesick at times

for the simpler life in America. In addition, Bill was writing and asking me to consider returning to be with him.

Having suffered personally and professionally through cholera, typhoid, and myocarditis and then measles, mumps, and the bubonic plague, I had serious questions about epidemics. I analyzed my questions and determined that if I knew the answers to those questions, I would likely have a master's degree in epidemiology. So I started looking into education possibilities for my next trip to the United States. I studied for the GRE and took the test in Dhaka. I was surprised, going into a proctored English exam, that the people waiting to take the test were all speaking only Bangla. The cheating was so flagrant in the exam room that it was easier to understand how they could manage such difficult English questions. I, myself, studied out of an English dictionary before the test, as I had not been speaking English on a regular basis for some time.

Mail was always a priority. Prayer letters were my communication with my prayer and support base back at home, and receiving mail was a highlight of any day. All my mail was opened as it came into the country. When the envelopes were glued back together, there was never any consideration given as to where to glue. The pictures people sent were often irretrievably stuck to the sides of the envelope. I learned later that people were actually assigned to read foreigners' mail to see what they were doing in the country. Any sensitive communication I sent out of Bangladesh was hand carried to ensure it got into the hands of my supporters. That news came as almost humorous, yet startling, piece of information. An ABWE missionary was asked at a restaurant, from someone he had never met, how his daughter was doing. He asked by her name. When the doctor asked how the stranger knew his daughters name, he explained that it was his job to read the missionary's mail.

As homesickness and exhaustion became increasing issues, the letters that came from Bill were more and more enticing. He wanted me to marry him. His letters were full of adoration and plans for a life together. I had declined before, but now I started to consider what life would be like married with a home and children of my own. Bill started planning a trip to Bangladesh, to come and rescue me like a maiden in distress. Until that point, my life plans were all of Bangladesh. I did not know what to think. Other people made a lot of plans for me while I was away. My mom and Bill's mother were friends. They were excitedly talking of the possibilities. Mom let Bill know how to contact me in Bangladesh. I started to get phone calls when I would go to Khulna for Bible study.

Of course, I thought of marriage too. Bill was not the first person to ask me to marry him. I had turned down other offers before. Even in Bangladesh, there were some choices to mull over. In a nation where marriages are often arranged, good missionary friends were considering options for me. An Iranian-Christian brother was a friend of mine. Some well-intentioned friends asked what I thought of him, but having a convert from Islam and UNHCR-certified refugee for a husband seemed complicated. Boby, the headmaster for HOJ school, was a dear Bengali friend. We spent endless hours working together closely and enjoyed each other's company immensely. He was single and considering marriage. A previous HOJ missionary had married a local Bengali Christian man. People in town and at the church in Khulna thought it was just a matter of time for Boby and me. We actually discussed the possibility, but I encouraged him to go ahead with a marriage arrangement with a fine girl from Chittagong. There was a young, single missionary man, who lived in another part of the country. I knew him well and occasionally daydreamed about him, but often when we were able to get together, the social pressure was so awkward we could barely connect.

Each of my trips into and out of Bangladesh had its own set of miracles and adventures wrapped up in them. As far as I knew, this was to be my last trip out. It had a flavor all its own too, much of it romance-related. In the end, I have to say I caved in to loneliness. Bill came to Bangladesh, excited to take me home and marry me, his intrepid missionary. The HOJ children had understood my leaving a couple of years earlier, because I was so sick. Actually, my leaving this time made perfect sense to them as well. In Bangladesh, it is unthinkable for a girl to still be unmarried at twenty-seven. To help them better understand my reason for leaving, and not have it feel like another abandonment, we had a reception-style party for the children at the orphanage. With many tears and confused emotions, I got on a plane with Bill.

We went straight to Texas, where I was surprised to find that people there were much further along in the wedding plans than I was. I had agreed to come spend time with Bill and to consider the option of marriage. Nan Walter helped me through many teary conversations trying to decipher God's will for my life and how to proceed, both before I left and after. She was always wise and gave friendly, godly counsel. I was confused, awkward, and forever feeling the pull of Bangladesh. Bill and I spent a few days together discussing life goals and walking hand in hand. Then he took me to Baylor University campus to check out their epidemiology degree options. As we walked along, he lamented that he could not hold my hand as he was in his army uniform. Having been in a Muslim country for years, this was quite easy for me to understand, since men and women don't hold hands there. He went on to say that if a cadet on the campus were to see him holding hands while in the captain's uniform, it would be inappropriate. "To a cadet, a captain is like a god."

I was uncomfortable with his comment and replied, "A captain is a captain, and only God is God." Then, *it* happened. A cadet walked by. That is it. Just walked by and did not salute. Bill seemed incensed at the affront of not being recognized for his status. He had no idea how that would affect me—nor did I. When he called the young man on it, I gasped and felt like I had been punched in the stomach. By the time the embarrassed cadet was on his way back to class, I was in tears. Bill tried to explain, saying, "What if someone of status in your profession was with me?" I told him of the humility of being in the presence of Mother Teresa just months before. To some, she was actually heralded as a living saint. I had been surrounded by the oppressiveness of the caste system★ for several years. I despised the social structure and injustice of the caste system and was seeing it displayed in the military setting. It literally turned my stomach and helped me make a decision right that moment. Bill tried to explain or retract, frantic to fix what seemed to have broken. I saw that I didn't fit there either, and I was ready to go home to Washington to see my family. I never spoke to Bill again.

Back home in Washington, it was wonderful to see my friends and family, despite a sense of embarrassment. I had thought I would marry him, or I wouldn't have come back at all. When I talked to my sister about Bill's behavior during my time in Texas, she agreed that he was not the right guy for me. Now that I was in the United States, I planned to get that master's degree before returning to Bangladesh. I had done well on the GRE. Between my education and experience background, I could get into any school. I applied to the one that interested me most, Tulane University in New Orleans, Louisiana. I felt at peace with the decision not to marry. There was confidence in my soul that if I were never to marry, I would be satisfied with my role being married only to Christ.

Then I met Richard Flatt. He was also a missionary home from the mission field. He was having visa problems and had returned to Spokane while his paperwork was being sorted out in Scotland. His parents and my mother were both on the missions' committee at Northview Bible Church. They suggested we get together to pray, as not many people understood being homesick for a place that was technically not home at all. After a couple of tries, we got to connect. From that day on, we met every day. We enjoyed our time as we prayed for the people God had given to our hearts. We talked of ministry challenges and rewards. We became fast friends. It was like meeting a spiritual twin. Richard was kind and handsome, but I had just let loose of Bill and any thoughts of marriage. We were just friends as we planned for our respective mission fields. I assured my sister, Valerie, that we were just "friends"—but she knew Richard too. Her view of the friendship was a sideways compliment: "He is such a nerd, Jill. He is perfect for you."

For the few months between acceptance and moving to grad school, I took a summer job as the nurse at Camp Sweyolakan again. I was comfortably back on a planned path. Sweyolakan is a resident camp. I moved out there for the summer in early June.

We would get a break for just one day a week. We could go home on a Monday afternoon to return to camp by Tuesday morning. Each Monday, Richard would come to the camp landing on Lake Couer d'Alene to come spend the afternoon with me. He sent me letters and mailed cookies to camp for me. In one letter, he referred to me as the Proverbs 31 woman. Working in Christian settings for many years, I knew that meant he was thinking of marriage. Every man would want to marry the Proverbs 31 woman. The proposal took me by surprise. As we were driving back to Spokane, he asked, "Well, what do you think?" I was puzzled. Think about what? Turns out that was his proposal. I stuttered and panicked while he tried to backpedal, saying, "It's okay … we'll just go get the fish." We were on our way to the grocery store at the time. We revisited the conversation later, and again and again. I had not realized we had "that kind" of relationship. My thoughts after telling Bill no were to get the degree and go back to Bangladesh. I couldn't imagine life outside that plan. It was a strangely difficult decision as the love of my life was a nation.

Scotland plans ruled Richard's thoughts, just as Bangladesh did mine. In Scotland, I was told, there were thousands of Bengalis with no Christian witness directed among them. As we tried to make plans, we saw the possibility of a life together on the mission field—still working with Bengalis, but in Scotland. It took me nearly a month of prayer and fasting, tears and conversations with God and others trying to decipher God's will for my life.

During a two-week session of camp, only a four-hour break was scheduled. Richard came to the landing to get me and take me out for dinner. I had plans to give him an answer to his question from the previous month. On that four-hour break, we got engaged. The whole process showed the hand of the Lord clearly. In fact, engraved in Richard's wedding band is Ephesians 3:20—God did more than we thought to ask or imagine.

On October 14, 1995, I married Richard Flatt. It was a wedding unlike any I had seen before. Hundreds of people attended. We were familiar to many people as missionaries only. I was far more known by my prayer letters than my presence. To honor that and bring people into the celebration of the life we planned together, we had a Scottish and Bengali theme. The bridesmaids—my sister, Valerie; Richard's sister, Mary; Starla; and my good college friend Heidi—wore red plaids. My beautiful red silk bridal sari, which I had worn to the reception-style party at Home of Joy, was artfully draped over the pulpit. The Walters came from their furlough in Michigan and sang *Household of Faith*. Elizabeth, from the SPU SPRINT team, also sang in the wedding, as did Cindy, our old roommate, who I had called from

Bangladesh when Starla needed our help. A traditional wedding gift in Bangladesh, a water jug, was filled with white orchids. A bagpiper played *Scotland the Brave* as we went down the aisle. At the reception we served Bengali *rosha golab* sweets and Scottish shortbread, along with the traditional wedding cake. A junior groom dressed in a kilt and a junior bride in a red sari. My father walked me down the aisle, but Starla emotionally gave over the responsibility of for caring for me to Richard. She explained to him, "When she needs a nap ... if ... she is sick ..."

We were excited, in love, and full of plans. We went right away to Scotland to be introduced to my new life. Though I was enjoying my time with Richard, I did not really enjoy Scotland much at all. It was so cold and not at all like Bangladesh. He did not get the paperwork he needed, and we actually had to pack up his things to return to America. We returned together, unsure of what would come next—but we were in it together now.

> Never concede to doing something so small that it could be accomplished entirely in your lifetime. Be a part of something that began before you were born, and will continue onward toward the fulfillment of all that God has purposed to accomplish.
>
> —Ralph Winter[9]

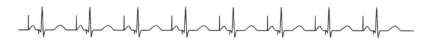

125

CHAPTER 11

Life Goes On

We share in his sufferings in order that we may also share in his glory. I consider that our present sufferings are not worth comparing with the glory that will be revealed in us.

—Romans 8:17b-18

Only three months after our wedding, I began having some serious heart problems again. I was afraid to even acknowledge it or to face it at all. I felt like an absolute fraud having really had no idea of the damage that was done internally through the struggle with myocarditis. I thought I had gotten away unscathed, but that was not the case. We had moved to Portland, Oregon, for Richard to finish his degree in youth ministry at Multnomah Bible College. The Youth for Christ Scotland staff continued to work on his visa processing. My heart was racing and stuttering, and it was difficult to breathe again. After some time, I went to a cardiologist and started some medications to try to slow down my heart.

Stress was overwhelming for a season. As newlyweds, we barely knew each other. He had asked me to marry him only six weeks after we met. We dated once a week through the summer and got engaged on a four-hour break from camp. I had not spoken English regularly for years and hadn't wanted to. I had not experienced a winter in years either, and winter 1995 was a severe one in Portland. My heart was out of control again. I cried all the time, wondering what I had done. Eventually, I was covered with hives too. All the while, we were planning to move to Scotland.

I worked to support us while he was in school. It was hard to get a job at first, as I had not worked in the United States for much of the previous five years. Equipment had changed. Medications had changed. One nurse manager recognized that my background as a missionary would prepare me to be innovative and flexible. I went to work at a little osteopathic hospital in Portland. The highlight of my job there was a new friend, Lynn Gibson, who was much needed. She saw my newlywed struggles and broken heart and took me under her wing. She would offer her little boy for puddle stomping therapy or quiet visits for tea as I needed.

It likely wouldn't have been any better for us if we had gone straight to Bangladesh. I would have been the one completely at home, while he wouldn't have been able to communicate or get around. Ultimately, the visa didn't work out in Scotland. Richard was crushed. God may have worked out what was better for both of us, even though we couldn't see that at the time.

We agreed on pastoral ministry together wherever the Lord might lead. I had told him going into the marriage that I could live anywhere in the world, but I wanted to have a neighbor named Rohima. The Bengali neighbor has yet to happen thus far, eighteen years into our marriage. We moved to Merced, California, where Richard was the youth pastor at an Evangelical Free Church. We were learning a whole new way of ministry together. I enjoyed it very much, though I always missed Bangladesh. Richard encouraged me to visit so I could see the kids I missed so much before having a family of our own.

Spending just a few weeks in Bangladesh, during the summer of 1997, was so different than living there. There was no homesickness, knowing it was just a quick visit. It was a valuable time of closure and a healing balm to my soul. The kids at Home of Joy knew I had married. They thought my husband was the man they had met; but as Richard was not there, I didn't need to explain anything. I had wedding pictures to show them, but they didn't notice any difference. I got to hug them all and once again did a spiritual inventory, spending an hour with each child alone being sure their questions were answered. I wasn't running a clinic or doing anything administrative during my time there. No meetings, just saying good-byes and seeing people who meant so much to me. Though I had no plans for returning to Bangladesh soon, I did plan to come back sometime. Richard would be with me, and we would serve the Lord together.

In California, I connected with a job that I came to love so much. I was still working with the poor and needy. Golden Valley Health Center served the majority Hispanic population in Merced. We had clinics next to migrant farm worker camps. It was different than the refugee camps, but it still matched me well. I thrived there professionally. Over our four years there, I was promoted three times. As in Bangladesh, I had the job of overseeing many clinics, hiring people, and teaching. Back in Bangladesh, working with Faith gave me an excellent example for being a good people manager.

Working with the youth from the church was a joint effort. I mentored individual girls from the church the whole time we lived there. I poured myself into one girl, who learned well; she has gone into missions herself. Kristi Nelson is now a nanny for missionary families around the world, mixing her own love of children and missions. In an effort to give the girls godly role models to look up to as they developed their Christian walks, I started a historical "Women of Faith" presentation program. Once a month, I would have the girls over for an overnight Bible study program. I taught about a different Christian woman each month, including Corrie ten Boom, Amy Carmicheal, Gladys Aylward, and Fanny Crosby, among others. I did hours-long presentations showing that by learning about these women and emulating their lives, we ourselves could become more Christ-like. I studied these women in so much depth, I felt like I had walked with them.

Occasionally, I still had problems with my heart; however, sometimes it would seem resolved, so I eventually quit taking my medicines. I had them, but if I felt fine, I would skip a day. A day would become a week and stretch from there. This continued until again, the rhythms were uncontrolled, and I had to go back to a cardiologist and get help. In Merced, for the first time, after many echocardiograms, the test showed that my heart valves were not holding up well anymore.

Getting pregnant with our first child was a time of excitement. Though I was considered high risk, the pregnancy went fairly smoothly. But our son wasn't growing too well, being medicated inside me by my beta-blockers. The last month I stopped taking the medications and let my heart run wild so my baby could grow like he needed. Graham Jeffrey was born on May 16, 1999, at 6lb 7oz and healthy. He grew very quickly once he was removed from the beta-blocker bath. We had our perfect jobs, perfect house, and perfect baby. We were very blessed. No foreign agency would have allowed me to stay in Bangladesh to have children because of the risks. We knew of some long-term ministry options that included Bangladesh, and I was patient and content.

We returned to Multnomah in Portland, Oregon, in 2002 so Richard could work toward his masters' degree while he pastored as the English pastor at a Korean church. In answer to our prayer, God blessed us with another baby while we were there. The second pregnancy was considerably more difficult than the first. God gave me a blessing-in-the-details to make it smoother: Lynn was my supervisor at work again. I was able to keep working as she kept a close watch over me. On days when she saw I wasn't doing as well, she would take my place and send me home. She guarded me through the pregnancy and even watched Graham when we went to deliver the baby.

Instead of being able to take less medication toward the end of the pregnancy, I eventually needed up to ten times the amount I had been taking. Every trip to the obstetrician she had to do an ultrasound, because she could never find the baby's heartbeat since mine was faster. Though Grace wasn't due until February 23, I timidly requested to be induced by Christmas. I had problems with breathing, heart rhythms, swelling, and low blood pressure the whole time I was pregnant. Grace Paulina came prematurely on January 6, 2003, without being induced. She was a tiny 5lb 12oz, but healthy. My doctor had strongly advised against the pregnancy, even recommending termination. She was right in that there was more damage to my heart because of the pregnancy, but I have never regretted my beautiful daughter who brings us so much joy.

We moved back to California after graduation. Richard became the associate pastor at Weed Berean Church. I worked in intensive care at Mt. Shasta hospital. When I was in Mt Shasta, I experienced my seventh encounter with heart failure. It seemed worse than all the previous ones. Every time it crept up on me, it was harder to recover from. I seemed to fall harder and get up slower. My heart didn't tolerate two hundred beats a minute for as long a time as the years went by. An echocardiogram showed that my ejection fraction was decreased to 40 percent and all my valves were leaking. It was a struggle to breathe at all at times. The long-term effects of having heart problems were having a cumulative effect.

Richard, Jill, Graham, and Grace Flatt

While the struggle was hard with my heart, God provided for me again, just what I needed. I worked with Debbie Hand, an experienced RN, who understood what was going on in my heart and was caring and supportive. She learned of the heart problem during one night to work, when she found me outside working hard to get some air. Another night, I arrived to work and realized my rhythms were not going to carry me through the night. She got me to the ER and was my nurse during my stay. Her kindness and concern were God's hands to me. It was time of terrible instability, as Richard's pastoral job was cut from the budget because of a crumbling economy and my health was eroding too. Debbie ministered to my soul, especially with her heart for missions. It gave me some comfort to pass on a mantle to her in some ways as I dealt with the growing realization that I may not be able to return to Bangladesh again at all.

Debbie invited me to come on a missions outreach with her. When Debbie and her husband, Larry, went to Panama to visit and help her missionary sister, I helped to prepare her. As she was leaving I gave her a financial gift, which surprised her. She said she didn't need money for her trip. I explained that it wasn't actually for her. She needed to find where it could be used to bless God's people in Panama. I tasked her with listening for God's voice to deliver His gift to His people.

While Debbie was deep in the jungle, she wondered what she was supposed to purchase for the needy Kuna tribal people she had come to serve. Shopping was scarce in the jungle. It came to light that there was a real need to buy goats to provide milk for the babies as they were weaned from nursing. When Debbie inquired about the cost, she found that it was the amount of money I had given. It was such a joy to be able to share in the blessing. The Kuna people were blessed—and so was my dear friend—by seeing the hand of God.

We were in the planning stages of a trip together to Asia when the heart problems came up again. Our trip is still on hold.

Sitting in my car writing a note to Debbie one day, God spoke to me again through the Scripture. The verse that I clung to from Philippians 4:13 (NASB) about "I can do all things through Christ who strengthens me," came to be stretched in a new way. Though I had known the verse nearly all my life, the verse that follows it had never struck me before. Paul says in verse 14, "but it was good of you to join me."

"I can do all things through Christ who gives me strength" (Philippians 4:13). For years I stood on that verse. It was my reason to have *no* doubt going into anything. There was always a feeling of nothing being beyond me. Paul spelled it all out for me: *all* things. It wasn't until the crisis in Mt. Shasta in 2006 that I noticed the next verse—and it touched my life. Bold, brave Paul said it to the people dear to him—in a quiet voice, I imagine— maybe even with a crack in his voice. He said, "But it was good of you to join me in my struggle" (Philippians 4:14).

Paul could do it—and for the glory of God, he would— but having the people who loved him come alongside in the difficult times made all the difference. The two beautiful verses are inseparable in my world now. Debbie was God's gift to me. It was good of God to give her to me, to join me in my struggle.

Another event occurred while we were ministering in Weed where I got to see God flex again. I served as the missions' teacher for the vacation Bible school program at church. The church staff said if I would teach it, the missions offering could go anywhere I wanted it too. Seeking God's desire, I decided that the money would be a "Send Annee to Bible School" fund. I even challenged the church with a matching amount. I would double any donations to make the mark more attainable. Annee was the godly little girl from Home of Joy in Khulna. She had wanted to be a "Bible woman," as lady teachers of God's Word are called in

Bangladesh. First, Annee would need Bible training. I spent the whole week teaching about her life and relationship with Christ. As I taught about Annee, I also explained other aspects of life in Bangladesh, including the situation of women, the persecuted church, and the religion of Islam. When I pulled it all together for the congregation, I burst into tears connecting those lessons to my Annee. The material was intended to challenge the very young people that they were not too young to have that kind of intimacy with Christ.

There was no Bible school near Khulna. For Annee, going to school would mean having to leave the orphanage and live elsewhere. All were blessed to hear of a real time, real life Christian. Though the stories of William Carey and Hudson Taylor continue to bless, I tried to make my story more current and applicable. The amazing part was that immediately after sending the money we collected for Annee to go to Bible school, a Bible school opened in Khulna. She got to stay at home and still go to school. Because the funds had been doubled, another girl at HOJ, Diba, was also able to attend. The blessings were as much mine and my church's as they were for Annee, Diba, and the Bengalis that would hear of Christ through them.

Richard's job in Weed had been trimmed from the church's budget as the economy crumbled. My health was faltering and we were on unsure footing. We were in "the deep end" again. Though it can be difficult, there is a real blessing in knowing that all successes are from the Lord. There was no mistaking that we were beyond ourselves and depending on the Lord. We couldn't "touch bottom," and there was nothing to cling to but Jesus and each other. I thought on many occasions about God giving us only what we can handle. I have also thought I must have been grossly overestimated. There were new lessons in providing daily strength and learning to depend on Him minute by minute with no reserve left in the tank.

We moved to the Blue Mountains in the eastern Oregon wilderness in 2006. Richard was realizing a dream of becoming a senior pastor. At a tiny church in a tiny town, we lived in the parsonage and got involved in small town life. Graham was the twenty-fourth student at the pre-K through senior high school when we moved there.

Unfortunately, my heart problems were quickly getting increasingly problematic. Going to the doctor repeatedly, more and more medicine was added. I was no longer taking a pill or two every day for the heart problems. I reached a peak, taking forty pills a day, and still the rhythms could not be controlled. I would wake up with a rate in the 160s and it would rise from there. I was wearing a King of Hearts monitor to help the doctors see what the rhythms were that were causing the problems, which were happening every day. The advice was given not to do the activities that caused the rhythm problems. That was everything. I tried to avoid the 200-plus tachycardia if I could.

Wearing the monitor was getting wearisome. I asked my dear friend Linda Hunt, from our church, to go on a walk with me with the full intention of not being careful. I planned to just get the rhythm they needed to see recorded and be done with the monitoring. Linda was God's provision to me in that lonely little town. She was either brave enough, or didn't know better, to volunteer to walk with me. As we walked, my heart was speeding up significantly. Then it was like changing gears, and the rhythm completely ran away. The monitor I was wearing said my heart rate was 264. I pressed the record button and we turned back toward home. She wondered if I was okay to walk home at all, but I just pressed on.

The phone call to transmit the rhythm strips went differently than usual. Generally, the answering service would receive the transmission and tell me they would get it to my doctor. This time, they gasped … "When was this? Are you all right? Hold the line!" I was on the phone for two hours, sending rhythm strips repeatedly. It was determined that the rhythms I was experiencing when I felt them run away were, in fact, not sustainable. If our town had not been so remote I would have gone to the hospital, but it was too far away to be of help. The doctor went through my backpack of medications with me on the phone telling me what medicine to take. He even talked me through giving myself a carotid massage, and then there was more transmitting rhythm strips—one after another. By the time I got off the phone, I had an appointment in Bend, Oregon, with an electrophysiologist.

Having been a nurse for so long, I felt sure I knew what I wanted and I didn't want for emergency care. I'd had to attempt to resuscitate (coded) many people with CPR over the years and was certain that I did not want that for myself. I had discussed getting a tattoo on my sternum to make it abundantly clear that I did not want those interventions. Richard was not as convinced. He was not keen on becoming a single father. Though I really didn't relish the idea, I agreed to surgery to try to correct the rhythms. The electrophysiologist did a cardiac ablation in Portland on my fortieth birthday. Cardiac ablation is a procedure that is used to destroy small areas in the heart that may be causing the heart rhythm problems. It was minimally successful. As soon as I was out of the electrophysiology lab where the procedure was done, they called a code on the next person in there. That was a scary, unsafe feeling. Also, I was actually discharged with a medication error. My already sky-high dosage of beta-blockers was inadvertently doubled. I had blood pressure problems for the next couple of months like never before; it would fall so low I could barely stand. The rhythms were barely controlled even though I was taking obscene amounts of cardiac medicines.

I had come to an impasse. Though the heart problems had plagued me for years, it was approaching the point of intervene or die. I took the kids and went to Spokane, where my parents and good cardiac care were available, leaving Richard at church in Oregon. I needed to be nearer to cardiac care.

There were murmurings among the church board about my leaving during vacation Bible school. Richard was in a lose/lose situation, but I had no option of putting off the doctors at this point. If he went with me, he was a bad pastor; if he let me go alone, he was a bad husband. He got to hear "Hasn't she had this for a long time. Does this really have to interfere with VBS?" I had been hurt in ministry before, but nothing was so painful as those times. It was a realization that the week-long summer Bible program mattered more to some people than if I lived or died.

While I struggled with the situation I was in, my old friends who knew me well were a great encouragement to me. Nan Walter, still in Bangladesh, helped me process this new chapter in my life—as she had so many others. There were some people who I reconnected with. I wanted to stay away from new people and having to explain my situation. I chose to stay in the safety of the people who understood.

While in Spokane, I connected with a friend back at Northview Bible Church, our parent's church. Bernice had married John Ellis, an old friend I had gone to school with since kindergarten. John had just discovered a tumor on his back, plunging him into a second battle with cancer and an uncertain future. Like me, the Ellis family was reeling and trying to rest in the Lord.

I had gone downstairs at the church to check Graham and Grace into Sunday school. Bernice and John saw me looking at the stairs, daunted at having to go up again with my rhythms in a frenzy. We sat together downstairs instead of going back up for the sermon and visited and prayed together. That reconnection bonded us for the trials that lay ahead. We kept each other current with updates on our health situations and prayed regularly for each other. Many emails and phone calls were exchanged to lift each other up from then on.

We marveled at the Scripture where God saves our tears, as each is so precious to Him. "You keep track of all my sorrows. You have collected all my tears in your bottle. You have recorded each one in your book" (Psalm 56:8, NLT). Bernice invited me, when we get to heaven, to come and swim with her in those tears. She commented, "As for a bottle, at this point, I'll have my own ocean!" For both of us, there were many tears yet to come. We agreed that if her tears were the Pacific Ocean, mine were the Indian Ocean.

God promises not give us more than we can handle. I have been occasionally shocked at how much He thinks I can handle. It does absolutely teach us to depend on Him for the *moment*. There is no way we have the reserves to handle some of the things that come our way. Hallelujah that we have Him to lean on and indeed to carry us when can no longer manage on our own. So often my prayer is for God to go behind me and before me and beside me. (He can because He is omnipresent.) I need for Him to go before me where I am afraid to go myself. I need Him to take the rear and protect me. I need Him to be with me and hold my hand for comfort as I go.

With some hesitation, I agreed to give the Portland electrophysiologist another chance. The second ablation was done a few months later. The doctor did so many burns, I felt like I had been put through a cheese grater. I also felt like I had fulfilled my obligation of trying to fix the problem. So far I had been able to avoid getting a rib spreader used on me, which was a relief. I didn't really want any open-heart surgery if I could avoid it. I announced that I was done volunteering to go back to the OR for more surgery. I said I would only have more surgery if I woke up and it was already done.

The hardest part of each procedure was the preparation and anticipation. I had to be free of the medications that would slow my heart down so they could find the electrical pathways of the rhythms that needed intervention. It was so unnerving to have to just let the rhythm go wild without taking any medication—especially now that I knew what they were doing to my heart function and that they were not sustainable. I was off work for months while they tried to work out the constant rhythm and pressure problems. Of course, I wondered if it would ever be better at all again. I struggled physically, emotionally, and spiritually really trying to deal with what life had become.

Besides leaning on the Scripture, music really ministered to my broken heart. Sometimes, my Bible reading times amounted to just tears rolling down my cheeks. A song by Casting Crowns helped me speak my heart to God, when my words no longer worked.

"Praise You in This Storm"

I was sure by now
God You would have reached down
And wiped our tears away
Stepped in and saved the day
But once again, I say "Amen," and it's still raining

As the thunder rolls
I barely hear Your whisper through the rain
"I'm with you"
And as Your mercy falls
I raise my hands and praise the God who gives
And takes away

[Chorus]
And I'll praise You in this storm
And I will lift my hands
For You are who You are
No matter where I am
And every tear I've cried
You hold in Your hand
You never left my side
And though my heart is torn
I will praise You in this storm[10]

I struggled so much that God, who had always been "above
and beyond what I could ask or imagine" (Ephesians 3:20) had
found *this* to be the best plan for my life. I do find it difficult at
times to rejoice in all circumstances, but I remind myself of what
I know instead of what I feel. He *is* actually still in control and has
not lost His grip at all—not in my beloved Bangladesh or even in
my own physical heart. It has definitely been a spiritual journey
as much as anything else. I can't say it isn't fair. Of course, it has
nothing to do with fairness. Believing in the Bible, I have no
option to pick and choose which parts I like or which I don't want
to include in my personal theology. Being the pastor's wife in our
little town, I didn't want people to look at me and think of God
as letting me down. God is God and He does what is best—or, at

the very least, He can make something even of the rubble in our lives. There are certainly days when I can't hold a rhythm and can't catch a breath that I think, *"Take me now, Lord."*

I had my own dream job in Oregon while Richard had his. I was the Director of Infection Control at Blue Mountain Hospital. I loved my job and my coworkers. They were so kind and helpful as my world unwound. Jodi Ritter, a fellow RN, was another godly woman who was God's gift to me during that time. I returned to work after the ablations, after being gone several months, still struggling with my heart rhythms. Jodi was there to make sure I was cared for and safe. My first night back at work, she left word with the other nursing staff that she was waiting at home to come take my place if needed. When I had to spend a stretch of days away from home at the hospital, Jodi opened her guest room to me. Sometimes, work was all I could do, and I had nothing left even for the drive home.

Our time in eastern Oregon came to a brutally painful and abrupt end. The chairman of the church board called Richard for an impromptu meeting. They had discussed some things in our absence and decided to ask for his resignation. With no warning at all, he was fired from his dream job. For pastor appreciation, they had just sent us on a fantastic trip to Hawaii. The church was growing. It made no sense, but really it was probably the only way to get us to move away. I would have never asked Richard to leave myself. I would have never said "medically, it is not safe for me here," as I did not want to do that to him. We immediately moved back to Spokane. After taking our children to Washington, Richard and I returned for more of our things. He left to take them home, while I stayed with Jodi to finish out my job properly.

That day—at work, with Richard having gone back to Washington—I finally really did collapse. That was the day when my coworkers' care for me extended beyond checking on how I was doing.

I knew that the newest medications were finally slowing down my heart. I came to the realization that it might be too much. No amount of any medicine to that point had been able to slow me down. I let my coworkers know that I might be in some trouble. Nancy, another RN, had asked me to come and work out in front of them instead of in my infection control office. I was so absorbed in what I was doing that more time just went by while the problem got worse and worse. Eventually, with my hands and face numb, and my heart barely beating, I knew time was short before I had to get out to them. I still didn't even think to stop my work. I grabbed what I needed to continue working at the nursing station and walked out to join them. As soon as I placed my papers down on the table, I collapsed into a heap. I hit my head and seized. When Nancy checked my pulse, there was none. My precious coworkers made quick work of saving my life.

I awoke in my own hospital's emergency room, with my own friends standing over me, some with tears running down their faces. They knew Richard was in Washington, they knew the whole situation, and asked if they could call anyone for me. Linda came all the way from Long Creek to sit with me in intensive care and hold my hand. None of the other people in the town from the church—people who were supposed to love us—cared at all that I had literally dropped dead at work. I was so hurt. I often wished I had been packing at the parsonage when it had happened. They would have found me dead then, and it would have been their problem to have to deal with. Jodi, who was not on duty that Sunday morning, came to be with me too. I was well cared for at Blue Mountain Hospital, being on the *wrong* side of the bed rails.

The hospital staff was able to reach Richard's family. The news was relayed to him as he picked up Grace from Sunday school at Calvary Chapel Spokane. He hurriedly took Graham and Grace to his parents and raced back to be with me. It was during the snowstorm of the century. The roads were nearly impassable, but Richard drove straight through. My sister, Val, and her husband, Steve, flew up from Phoenix to be with us. My family took tender, loving care of me. My gentle son, only eight years old, was aware of something going on and frightened. Four-year-old Grace was blissfully oblivious.

Our move to Spokane was complicated by weather, health, and broken emotions. My heart really was broken. When we took the last load of our belongings out of the county, Richard stopped the truck at the side of the road. We got out and shook the dirt off our feet. If he had known where more shoes were in the truck, he likely would have thrown the shoes away there.

A cardiologist in Spokane examined me, and I was quickly fitted with a Medtronic pacemaker. Starla came when I had that done, to be my arms for me while I couldn't lift anything. Just like in the typhoid sepsis days, she ministered to me in my time of need. The doctor's appointments were unending. Richard could not find a job, so I was working to support us. Once again I collapsed, this time in the emergency department where I worked at Sacred Heart Hospital. I'd gone to take a quick break and was hauled out of the changing room on a gurney.

It took us a while to get back to speed. Spiritually, we were spinning. Emotionally, we were devastated. Physically, I was broken. It was good to have our parents there with us to help. I never needed my mom so much as I did during these days in my early forties.

The driving theme verse of my life changed over these years from the victorious Psalm 37:4, "Delight yourself in the Lord," to Psalm 34:18, "The Lord is close to the brokenhearted and saves those who are crushed in spirit." The idea of the Lord drawing close to the brokenhearted has meant so much to me. Most of the time, I am not terribly upset with the things that have happened in my life. The heart problem turned out to be more life-changing than I ever imagined it would be. Life is no longer a victorious feeling, but at times it is a struggle to live. I have not for a moment in this process doubted God or His power or His sovereignty, but maybe—on occasion—I have wondered about His plan. I have, at times, felt very alone on the journey. Although, I am confident that the one set of "footprints" is not mine; I have, indeed, been carried. I have been thoroughly out of strength, or at least energy. It really is so important to me that even this be a part of my testimony. Even in the hardest and darkest hours, I have known that I am not on my own. That has made this journey easier than many other people's hard lives. I am blessed to be in this adventure with Christ. When people look at my life, I want them to see Jesus—no matter what the struggle might be from my part. He is not my fair-weather friend. William Borden, a missionary who gave his life in Egypt, stated it well: "No reserves. No retreats. No regrets." In my brokenness, I find that God is still there.

Life is not as much fun as living in the dream-come-true times of my Bangladesh years. Sometimes I read my Bible and just cry. I still hold out hope that things will improve enough that someday I will be able to take my family to see the land that I love so much. I still speak Bangla to God, as He is the only one here who can understand me.

I am still in contact with those back in Khulna at Home of Joy orphanage. In 2009, I received a devastating letter about Annee. She really had lived much of her life more connected to heaven than to earth. The God she loved so much called her home at twenty-three years old. She died instantly in a pedestrian versus car accident. In part, there was a feeling in me that ministry was being mantled by Annee, that she would carry it on. I knew she was there in Bangladesh for the long term, demonstrating by the way she lived what life with Christ could be like. The world seemed an emptier place with her gone, but I knew there was much rejoicing in heaven. Annee, who it seemed could always see God, was in His presence.

The Home of Joy is connected via Facebook now, like so much of the rest of the world. Looking at a "friend's friend," I noticed a picture of a familiar-looking Bengali girl. Her name was Jill, though Jill is not a Bengali name. I found out that after I moved away, Roma changed her name to mine. She apologized, but I just felt honored and reassured that I had made an impact in at least some lives. Many of the children have grown up and are walking with the Lord now. When I reconnected through Facebook with David from Home of Joy, he was grateful to have found "his childhood mother." I love that I get to be a part of their lives from so far away even now.

Looking back, I was considered so strong and so bold. I am not at all meek now, but certainly I'm not strong anymore. I relate to the old Rich Mullins song, "Hold Me Jesus." He sang,

> Hold me, Jesus, I'm shaking like a leaf.
> You have been my King of Glory,
> Won't you be my Prince of Peace?[11]

145

I have many times walked white-knuckled, holding the hand of my Savior as I tiptoe down the dark and scary path. I struggle seeing where God can use me. In His graciousness, He shows me again that He can still use me if I am willing. In California and Oregon, as my health failed, people took notice of how my relationship with the Lord affected how I coped with what was happening to my heart. Some people who came to call Jesus their Lord in part were influenced through my life. One was the gentle, kind nurse named Janie Bristow, who was there the night I collapsed at work. Shortly after that, she moved away. Later Janie called and let me know that my example helped lead her back to the Lord. That was all I had wanted, even when I was well. God used her to show me that I wasn't completely useless now. When I gave my life to Christ, it was for him to use as He saw fit. I left no caveat that it had to be checked through me for permission. I do not always understand, but I choose to trust Him still.

I know God can heal me, as I know He *can* do all things. I also firmly believe in the sovereignty of God. No *is* an answer to prayer. If God chooses to continue to use me in this way, it is my job just to serve Him well. I need the courage and grace to do it well. Where I used to have little fear of anything—except bats—going to doctors now terrifies me. For so many cardiology appointments, it seems I just got to hear more and more of what is going wrong. Once, I took a long, "leisurely" drive to the doctor from our home, and two hours later I still wasn't there yet. I sometimes cry at the prospect of just having to go into the office. It was much easier to serve in the role of missionary and in pastoral roles: busy, efficient, and dependable. I did not dream of this role, and it is an adjustment that I guess I still haven't fully come to terms with.

Because of my health difficulties, I struggled working the long hours in the busy emergency room at Sacred Heart. I transferred to the cardiac floor after only a few months. In that interview, they had said how glad they were that I would need so little training; I just had to learn about transplants and VADs (ventricular assist devices, also known as mechanical hearts).

My own MD, Dr. Ndirangu, had asked if I would consider a transplant myself. Working on the cardiac floor gave me a rare chance to see it all close up before having to make such a decision for myself. Though I knew and understood cardiology better than most nurses ever would, that turned out to be very hard at times, seeing people suffer and die from the same disease I struggle with. I learned that having a pacemaker was not enough to stop me from passing out on the floor, even in front of patients—especially if I had to do any work above my head, like hanging intravenous bags. I found this out when I was changing a clock and ended up on the floor after the world had turned dark again. I also discovered that I was more than a little traumatized when it came time to resuscitate people anymore. Many of the mechanical heart patients were also in the one-third of people who get myocarditis and struggle with its lasting sequelae. It became what my nightmares were made of.

As we settled in Spokane, we shuffled between a few churches. After being hurt so badly in Oregon, I was leery of people at church. I didn't want to be seen as broken, so I did not connect with anybody at all. Richard was a bit quicker to regain his footing. After a couple of years, he volunteered for us to host a small group Bible study. We plugged in again at Turning Point Open Bible Church. God is flexing again, making Himself known in our world.

As of 2013, Richard is involved as the recovery and visitation pastor at Turning Point Open Bible, although not in a staff position. He worked for three difficult years at Taco Bell before getting a job in sales at Batteries+Bulbs just this year. He was also exhausted and defeated through much of this rocky journey, some of which turned out to be medical problems of his own. When we thought we couldn't take another thing, Richard was diagnosed with colon cancer, which God graciously took away. I learned at that juncture that God was indeed enabling me to deal with what I had on my plate—because once we added cancer to the mix, I got to see how I really couldn't take that much more. When the surgeon went to remove it, the cancer could not be located. We left the hospital confused and thanking God. I even knew at that point to thank God that we only had to deal with myocarditis, lupus for Richard, and the associated medical debt— but *not* cancer too.

Graham, in high school now, dreams of being a herpetologist; he has eleven reptiles in his bedroom already. He may yet want to visit Bangladesh after all. Grace is still blissfully oblivious at ten years old. She wakes up singing and goes to sleep singing. She takes drama and voice lessons, even in just the fifth grade. She is a social butterfly that loves every person she meets, and they all love her.

God provided a way out of my sometimes scary cardiology job this year. To help me last longer as a nurse, I thought I should get away from the floor nursing. I found an interesting job where I could still use my cardiology knowledge, but not be as personally exposed to such terrifying daily reminders of myocarditis and what it means for me. Cardiac medical research is a way for me to use my knowledge while avoiding excessive exposure to the threat of illness and the constant reminder of the giant that wrecks such havoc in my world. Now, I have a chance to potentially help to find answers to the medical questions that could change my own life. I completely feel like a Medtronic girl and have a great opportunity to contribute to the knowledge that has changed my own life- for both cardiac drugs and devices. I, rather tongue in cheek, tell my electrophysiologist that I recommend a pacemaker to everyone, because they are that great.

While journeying down this new road, I'm trying to remember to look at the Savior and not at the path, keeping my gaze fixed on Jesus. I don't need to see the next step, because I can't make it there on my own anyway. I just keep looking up and am amazed that somehow I get from point A to point B. God has continued to show Himself faithful and present. Hudson Taylor said, "All our difficulties are only platforms for the manifestations of His grace, power and love."[12] There can be joy in the dependence, recognizing where God has intervened in a powerful way—in the deep end.

My friend Bernice—whose husband, John, has "graduated" from this life, as she calls it—refers to it as an adventure with Christ. I used to say in my prayer letters that, "This life with Christ is certainly a joyous adventure." I know this adventure has not always been a joyous journey, but one of real fellowship of the suffering. The fellowship with Him, in whatever form, *is* reason to praise Him. "But to the degree that you share the sufferings of Christ, keep on rejoicing, so that also at the revelation of His glory you may rejoice with exultation" (1 Peter 4:13, NASB). Bernice has been faithful to both remind me of this gently and walk through the pain with me. We have been very blessed, even on this "bad" part of the adventure. The Lord has not left us nor will He forsake us!

I had prayed for my heart to be broken by the things that break the heart of God. It is broken now in ways I hadn't originally anticipated at all. God really did break my heart, or at least allow my heart to be broken. God gave me the kind of love for the Bangladeshis that He has for us. People said it was odd that it really did break my heart. I certainly never imagined that one infection would become a lifelong battle with heart problems. But God is sovereign, and long ago I gave Him full reign over my life. I'm not asking to take it back. I can't accept the good things from the Lord and expect to be exempted from the bad. Though I completely agree and understand "thy will be done," I do have occasional struggles, especially with fear. On the other side comes heaven, and there is no fear in that. There is certainly a new level of dependence—being literally dependent for every breath and every heartbeat at times. It is a new way of walking with the Lord. I cannot say it has been what I would have chosen. Sometimes my prayers are literally cries. I know God can handle my anger, frustrations, and fears. He is neither surprised nor threatened at all. He has big shoulders. Nothing I could throw at Him would be too much. I do need prayer to succeed in this new life, if this is to be it, and to have courage to face the changes as they come. The "adventure" has been terrifying at times, but the fellowship is sweet.

If I could have known the things that would come into my life, I wouldn't have changed it at all. Though I hadn't expected my heart to go through such difficulties, it was worth it. Bangladesh was a dream come true for me. All I wanted in life was to see Bengali hearts turn to Jesus. Someday, when I worship around the throne of God in heaven surrounded by peoples from all nations, some of them will be Bengali. Some of those hearts will be there because I was there to share the love of the Lord. It seems a worthwhile trade to me—my earthly heart for the Bengali eternal ones.

I have a broken heart and that is normal for me. It may never be healed this side of heaven. That's okay. God uses my broken heart to keep me close to Him; without it, I might not need Him so much.

—Carol Kent, *A New Kind of Normal*[13]

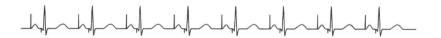

Others May, You Cannot

if anyone wishes to come after me, he
must deny himself and take up his
cross and follow me. for whoever wishes
to save his life will lose it; but whoever
loses his life for my sake will find it.
—matthew 16:24-25

If God has called you to be truly like Jesus in all your spirit, He will draw you into a life of crucifixion and humility. He will put on you such demands of obedience that you will not be allowed to follow other Christians. In many ways, He seems to let other good people do things which He will not let you do.

Others who seem to be very religious and useful may push themselves, pull wires, and scheme to carry out their plans, but you cannot. If you attempt it, you will meet with such failure and rebuke from the Lord as to make you sorely penitent. Others can brag about themselves, their work, their successes, their writings, but the Holy Spirit will not allow you to do any such thing. If you begin to do so, He will lead you into some deep mortification that will make you despise yourself and all your good works. Others will be allowed to succeed in making great sums of money, or having a legacy left to them, or in having luxuries, but God may supply you only on a day-to-day basis, because He wants you to have something far better than gold, a helpless dependence on Him and His unseen treasury.

The Lord may let others be honored and put forward while keeping you hidden in obscurity because He wants to produce some choice, fragrant fruit for His coming glory, which can only be produced in the shade. God may let others be great, but keep you small. He will let others do a work for Him and get the credit, but He will make you work and toil without knowing how much you are doing. Then, to make your work still more precious, He will let others get the credit for the work which you have done; this to teach you the message of the Cross, humility, and something of the value of being cloaked with His nature.

The Holy Spirit will put a strict watch on you, and with a jealous love rebuke you for careless words and feelings, or for wasting your time, which other Christians never seem distressed over. So make up your mind that God is an infinite Sovereign and has a right to do as He pleases with His own, and that He may not explain to you a thousand things which may puzzle your reason in His dealings with you. God will take you at your word. If you absolutely sell yourself to be His slave, He will wrap you up in a jealous love and let other people say and do many things that you cannot. Settle it forever; you are to deal directly with the Holy Spirit, He is to have the privilege of tying your tongue or chaining your hand or closing your eyes in ways which others are not dealt with. However, know this great secret of the Kingdom: When you are so completely possessed with the Living God that you are, in your secret heart, pleased and delighted over this peculiar, personal, private, jealous guardianship and management of the Holy Spirit over your life, you will have found the vestibule of heaven, the high calling of God.

—G. D. Watson (1845–1924)[14]

Appendices

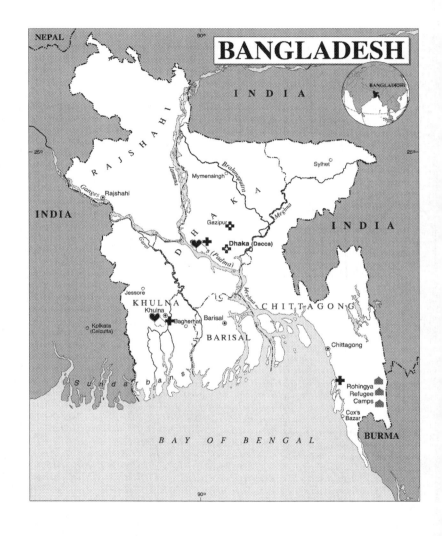

Medical Glossary

In this nontraditional appendix I will not just define some diseases, but I will also expound on how they relate to Bangladesh and even my own story.

cholera—Cholera is an infectious diarrheal disease caused by eating contaminated food or water (WebMD.com). Poorly nourished people sometimes die within twelve hours of the onset of diarrhea. It is characterized by "rice water" stools, as thin as water and just a bit cloudy. After water-related disasters, cholera epidemics often follow. Bangladesh gets more than its fair share of cyclones and floods. Because of this, the International Center for Cholera and Diarrheal Disease Research is located in Dhaka, Bangladesh. They maintain a hospital there dedicated solely to the treatment of diarrhea. If a patient needs hospitalization, they will not be turned away. In epidemics, cots are lined up outside under tarps. Oral rehydration therapy (ORT) was pioneered here and deaths by diarrhea have since decreased by 30 percent according to ICCDDRB. They lead the quest for "global lifesaving solutions."

encephalitis—Encephalitis is an acute infection and inflammation of the brain itself (WebMD.com). There can be many causes, but children, elderly, and the malnourished are most at risk. It can be a complication of other processes, including mumps.

malaria—Malaria is a communicable parasitic disorder caused by the bite of an infected anopheles mosquito. Worldwide, there are half a *billion* cases per year. Though the problem is considered greatest in sub-Saharan Africa, Asia also has a high incidence rate. It is characterized by a high fever, and it also often comes with a lifetime of reoccurrences. It can be wise, especially for short-term visits, to take malaria prevention pills when traveling to a malaria-infested area. Having public health or epidemiologists look at the incidence exactly where you are going is also important, as there is much medication resistance. Long-term use of the anti-malaria medications can have an adverse effect on vision.

malnutrition—Malnutrition is a major third-world problem. It is one of the areas that most grossly contrasts the developing world with the developed world. Besides a lack of food, worms and parasites also take a nutritional toll. The *QIMP* resource book states among Bangladeshi children, there are 95 percent with protein energy malnutrition (PEM). Among cases of PEM, there is a "wet malnutrition" known as *kwashiorkor* and a "dry malnutrition" called *pellagra* or *marasmus*. *Kwashiorkor* is a Swahili word for "second child"; this disorder is named after the tragedy of seeing the first child waste away after a new baby takes over being breastfed. PEM still causes the deaths of five million children annually. According to the World Health Organization (WHO), approximately 90 percent of children in the developing world are malnourished to some degree with 36 percent underweight, 43 percent stunted, and 10 percent wasted.

measles—Measles is a highly contagious viral infection. In America, it is rarely seen because of routine immunization. As Bangladesh develops, they are starting to catch up. According to recent WHO assessment, Bangladesh has reached almost 83 percent in measles immunization coverage. Center for Disease Research (CDC) research has determined that it takes at least 90 percent measles coverage to prevent outbreaks, and a single-dose vaccine is insufficient for measles prevention. Having a significant number of children die of measles is considered an indicator of third-world status. Measles is so highly infectious that in America a single case is flagged as an outbreak by the CDC and is treated very seriously. Working as a nurse back in the United States, I've had very few coworkers who have ever even seen an actual case of measles in our well-immunized nation.

mumps—Mumps is a contagious viral infection that causes painful swelling of the parotid glands, between the ear and jaw. Mumps can lead to hearing loss and meningitis. In older males, it can cause orchitis and occasionally fertility problems. Vaccine coverage is usually in combination with measles, mumps, and rubella as a three-injection series.

myocarditis—Myocarditis is an inflammation of the heart muscle tissue. There are several causes: viral, autoimmune, and others. After the infection and inflammation have abated, the immune system may continue to attack. It is a fairly rare disease, but it's more common in other areas of the world. Approximately one-third of the patients die, one-third recover, and the other one-third live with varying degrees of heart problems. Not surprisingly, and by God's grace, I learned more about this disease over the years as I struggled with its lifelong effects. It is one of the most common reasons to need heart transplant surgery. Where I now work, when people receive this diagnosis, I ache for them. I am most surprised when patients come in imminently needing a transplant from the disease, and they are not aware that they had it to begin with. After my doctor asked if I would ever get a transplant, I went to work on the transplant unit to investigate for myself. As of yet, I do not qualify and hope to never have to make that choice.

plague—This dreaded disease of the fourteenth century, known as the Black Death, caused the death of nearly one-third the population of Europe. It was not lost in history, however, and still pops up from time to time around the globe. The 1994 outbreak epicentered in Surat, India, and resulted in 693 cases and 56 deaths. In the two days following the first death, 300,000 people fled Surat in an absolute panic. It was the most unprecedented movement of people since the 1947 partition of India. There ensued a subcontinent panic of buying antibiotics. Getting the plague immunizations before leaving for rural Bangladesh was a real hassle, as there is little availability. I sure felt good about knowing I'd actually had the full vaccine series, though, when the plague struck India. I had gotten mildly ill from the vaccine while I was yet in nursing school. It was a real scare for people to even be close to a vaccine-induced mild case of the plague. I had to be authorized by the infection control department at the hospital to be allowed to finish my clinical rotations for the quarter.

scabies—Scabies is caused by a small mite that actually gets under the skin. It causes very itchy bumps that can appear all over the body, but most commonly start between the fingers and around the waist. The bugs travel more at night and move rapidly inward. As the entrance wounds are scratched, commonly with germ-laden fingernails, the skin is broken open and a super infection can occur. The sores become filled with pus, and sometimes fevers and swollen lymph nodes begin. Scabies spread easily and are difficult to treat. Antibiotics can treat the superinfection, but the tiny bugs can be daunting to stop. Personal cleanliness is significant for scabies eradication. In slums, refugee camps, orphanages, and other places where overcrowding and lower standards of living prevail, scabies thrive. Throughout Bangladesh, *pesra* (scabies) were considered more a norm than an illness, but left untreated, the infection can erode away good health completely. It was devastating to see people actually *die* from the complications of untreated scabies.

tetanus—Tetanus, also called "lockjaw," is virtually unseen in America, as it is another vaccine-preventable illness. While there are nearly one million cases annually worldwide, the immunized world sees only rare cases. It is a disease of deep anaerobic tissue origin. In developing countries, where shoes are not commonly worn, it is much more common. When the infection sets in, the bodies muscles go into deep tetany. The body is completely arched with all the muscles rigid often terminating with an inability to even breathe. Neonatal tetanus is seen when the umbilical cord is cut by an unclean instrument. Of the million annual cases, almost six hundred thousand are neonatal tetanus. In Bangladeshi villages, a sharpened piece of bamboo often severs the umbilical cord and starts the tetanus germs on their deadly path. Even in the developed world, 45 percent of patients will die. In the slum clinics, FOB handed out delivery kits to pregnant ladies that included a sterile razor blade and gauze for taking care of the cord if they were having the usual home delivery.

tuberculosis—Tuberculosis (TB) is a bacterial infection. It is most commonly found in the lungs, but it can occur in nearly every part of the body. It is also called "consumption" or the "wasting disease." In Bangladesh, as in much of Asia, it is very prevalent. It is one of the few truly airborne communicable diseases. TB can be a latent or active infection. It is a long, difficult, and expensive disease to treat. There is also more and more drug resistance against tuberculosis. HIV patients get a form of TB as well. Active pulmonary tuberculosis turns the grape-like structure for alveoli air exchange to more of a broccoli-looking formation that is not effective for gas exchange. Once the damage is done, the lung cannot restructure. When it is discovered, it takes six months to two years of several antibiotics for effective treatment. Extrapulmonary TB will show a positive skin test but negative chest X-ray. It can be hard to find, but the medical treatment is about the same. Overcrowding and poor sanitation affects TB transmission as well. A baseline state of malnourishment makes getting sicker more likely.

typhoid—Typhoid fever is a tropical illness also known as enteric fever. The bacteria are carried in dirty food and water, as is often the case. In the United States, less than five hundred cases per year occur, many of which are related to travel outside the country. Worldwide, five hundred thousand people die per year out of the estimated thirteen million people who contract the illness. Typhoid can be carried unknowingly, leading to new outbreaks. Approximately 3–5 percent of those inflicted become long-term carriers. "Typhoid Mary" is America's most famous case; she was a cook who infected many households over a decade in the early 1900s. The duration of the illness is four to six weeks, with many people dying in the three- to four-week time period. It is a serious, acute illness with many possible complications. A very high fever with relative bradycardia is often typhoid fever.

Catherine Marshall's book *Christie,* written about her mother's ministry years, tells the story of a typhoid epidemic in the American Appalachians. There are immunizations for typhoid fever prevention. The old three-shot series, which was only 50 percent effective, has been replaced by an oral vaccination, which is a bit more effective at closer to 70 percent.

worms—Parasites are organisms that live on or in a host and get their food at the expense of their host (cdc.gov). There are many kinds of helminth infestations. Ascariasis is the most common cause for intestinal blockages necessitating surgical intervention in the tropical world and the most common worm infestation worldwide. At the mission hospital in Bangladesh, many surgeries are done to fix complete intestinal blocks resultant from a tangled ball of worms. During the life cycle of the roundworm, they move back and forth from the GI system to the pulmonary system. Patients will sometimes vomit worms and other times cough them up. Worms contribute significantly to malnutrition problems. Valuable nutrients get utilized by the worms instead of their hosts. Hookworms feed off the blood, thereby making the host anemic. Skinny, malnourished people with big, round bellies are often full of worms. The treatment is easy and inexpensive for many types of worm infestations. There are some worms that are more difficult to control and can make a patient much sicker than others. Filariasis is a leading cause of permanent disability globally, causing elephantiasis.

xeropthalmia—Xerophthalmia is one of the world's leading causes of blindness, and it is completely preventable. In the third world, with its myriad problems with malnutrition, a lack of vitamin A can cause blindness. One capsule of vitamin A every six months is enough to thwart xerophthalmia. The disorder advances from dry eye to night blindness and eventually complete blindness and further morbidity related to vitamin deficiency. WHO statistics are that a million child deaths would be prevented annually by vitamin A nutriture. Though most easily recognized by the eye problems, vitamin A deficiency is a systemic problem that impacts morbidity and mortality. Bangladesh is one of thirty-nine nations identified as having serious xerophthalmia problems.

Most of the information in the medical glossary came from years of running clinics, nursing, infection control, and tragic personal experience. For further information, WebMd.com, cdc.gov, and a Taber's medical dictionary.

Bangla and Bangladeshi Culture Glossary

amulets—Small charms believed to have powers of magical or spiritual protection. In Bangladesh, "folk Islam" is prevalent. By distance and education, they are a long ways away from Saudi Arabia. There is a syncretistic mix of Islam, Hinduism, and animism. Children have these charms or trinkets tied around their necks, arms, and waists to protect them from evil spirits.

baby taxi—These are also known as "auto rickshaws." A very small motorized three-wheeled transport, like a motorcycle with a two-stroke engine and handlebars, but it also has a small body on the frame that is open on both sides. It is a vehicle for hire and rarely seen privately owned. Most of them are black and yellow with wild fringe and car decorations on the back.

baksheesh—The literal translation is *tip*. Baksheesh also means bribe in some arenas. Beggars all over South Asia have their hands out and pathetically say *baksheesh* while looking for alms to survive. Likewise, the same term can be heard going through customs or dealing with officials at times.

bideshi—The Bangla term for foreigners. Bengalis can see each other as male, female, young, and old, but the foreigners are simply *bideshis*. One friend from language school was out with his lovely British wife, who was wearing a sari. A Bengali man asked whether she was male or female. It is an interesting perspective from a Bengali point of view that all foreigners look alike.

burka—A burka is an article of women's clothing worn for observing the conservative Islamic practice of *purdah* (literally, curtain). The burka comes in several styles, but is usually an over-the-head and all-the-way-to-the-feet garment. There are varying degrees of face coverings, ranging from a light screen to a total visual block.

caste system—The caste system is a social structuring system based on heredity or birthright. The whole social system dictates what jobs a person can have and whom they can associate with. Many times in South Asia orphans will not be taken in, because their caste is unknown and people will not risk adopting outside their caste level. There are many levels in the Indian caste system, ranging from the priestly Brahmins to the Dalits (untouchables). There are approximately 160 million untouchables in India today. Though Bangladesh is a separate country, the social issues are often shared. Lower caste members face severe problems, such as segregation and violence against them (Wikipedia).

chele/meye—*Chele* is Bangla for boy and *meye* means girl. *Chelemeye* together means children. Living at orphanages in Bangladesh, there are important everyday, all-day long words.

ferryghat—An access point for crossing a river by boat. It is usually a toll point where travel cannot be continued without the roads. There are actually more navigable waterways than roads in Bangladesh.

hajj—The hajj is one of the five tenets of Islam. It is the annual pilgrimage to Mecca, where the faithful walk in circles around the holy Ka'aba. The cubical structure is considered the center of worship for the Islamic world. It is located inside the Grand Mosque in Mecca, Saudi Arabia. When Muslims pray, anywhere around the world, they face the Ka'aba in prayer. It is a goal for each faithful Muslim to go on the hajj at least once in their lifetime. The pilgrimage comes with lifelong respect and recognition. The person is then known as a haji. Often men dye their hair and beards red to show they have been on the pilgrimage.

hartal—A term used in the Indian subcontinent for a strike action (Wikipedia). It often involves a complete shutdown of workplaces, schools, businesses, roads, and government offices. Often, a hartal is "called" or planned by a certain political party. That party will enforce the hartal with violence, burning cars if they are on the roads or demolishing shops if they are found open. When one party calls a hartal, an opposition party will often call one as well to show their strength. The hartal is scheduled for certain hours and is a rather organized chaos. In Bangladesh, it is a common method of politics and very inconvenient for daily life. Where we have a campaign season in the United States, there is a hartal season as the elections draw near in Bangladesh.

Injil Sharif—The Injil Sharif is the Holy Law, the Bible, written for Muslims to understand. It is outlawed in many Islamic nations. While the Bible has been available in Bengali since the days of William Carey, it was only recently translated to make better sense for the Muslim people who use different words than the Hindus and Christians. There can be penalties for even being found with an Injil Sharif. Bangladesh is on the list put out by the World Watch of nations known to persecute Christians. Voice of the Martyrs also works in Bangladesh with persecuted Christians.

Jishu—*Jishu* is the name of Jesus in Bengali. His name is just as sweet in any language.

mashi—*Mashi* is a family term for a mother's sister. It is a close family relation. In the orphanage, we used the term for the room mothers.

Mukti Bahini—The Mukti Bahini were the heroic freedom fighters of the war for independence in Bangladesh. They were mostly ill-equipped and poorly armed civilians who fought against the Pakistani army. As the war for independence is a part of such recent history, the Mukti Bahini are still revered in Bangladesh culture.

nakshi kantha—*Nakshi kantha* is the national handicraft of Bangladesh. It is unique to this part of the world. It is most commonly done with old threads on old materials, but the Friends of Bangladesh Widow's Sewing Center does beautiful silk embroidery on silk background. The details of the embroidery work are intricate. Each piece can take months to work on, depending on the size of the piece, and is really a unique work of art.

neem—The neem tree is a deciduous tree that has several practical uses locally. It is in the mahogany family. In Swahili, the name of the tree means "the tree of the forty," as it is thought to treat forty different diseases. The leaves are used in making soap that is effective in the treatment of scabies. The Mennonite Central Committee made neem soap very reasonably priced so it would be accessible to people who needed it. Whenever I would travel from Dhaka to Khulna, I would bring a giant, heavy case of neem soap. Twigs off the neem tree are used throughout Bangladesh for cleaning teeth. Various parts of the neem tree are used as antibacterial, antiviral, antimalarials, antifungal, antihelminthic, antidiabetic, and much more.

rickshaw—The rickshaw is often known as the cycle rickshaw. A hard-working, low-paid person will cycle to pull people and equipment through Asia's traffic to earn a barely subsistence wage. Usually, the rickshaw is rented and the rickshaw wallah will have to make over a certain amount just to break even. The people-powered rickshaw, without even a bicycle, is much less common but is still seen in West Bengal, or Kolkata in India. There are about four hundred thousand cycle rickshaws in Dhaka.

Salwar-kameez— These are women's clothing generally considered more casual and often for younger women. It consists of very baggy pants and a long shirt that comes to at or even below the knees. For modesty sake, it is usually also worn with a scarf called an orna.

Shishu Bhavan—Children's Building (home). This is the name of Mother Teresa's orphanage in Kolkata.

taka—The monetary unit of Bangladesh. It is not an internationally recognized currency. In January 2011, the exchange rate was 71 taka per 1 US dollar. The average daily earning in Bangladesh is about a dollar a day. Prices have been rising far faster than people can keep up with, and what the taka can buy gets smaller and smaller. There are 100 poisha to the taka. Poisha are so worthless that banks do not deal in the smaller denominations, and if people give beggars poisha, the beggars will throw the money back.

trunk call—This term has no meaning outside of the Indian subcontinent or UK-affiliated nations. In India, a long-distance, operator-assisted phone call is called a trunk call. It is an older telecommunication system of sharing phone lines and having operators connect calls on the few available phone lines.

upazila—An *upazila* is a political breakdown of the Bangladesh landscape, like a county. There are six districts in Bangladesh, which are broken into upazilas.

vangari—A *vangari* is similar to a cycle rickshaw, but instead of having a seat in the back for a couple of people, there is a wooden platform. Sometimes people may sit on the back of a vangari, but more commonly they are used for the transport of goods. The platform is about four foot square. The vangari and rickshaw drivers are phenomenally strong.

Missions Appendix

Cornelia "Corrie" ten Book (1892–1983) was a Dutch Christian who bravely helped the secret underground resistance against the Nazis in World War II. After surviving Ravensbruck death camp, Corrie became a world-renowned Christian author and speaker, sharing her story of love overcoming hate and Christ's love. Her most famous book, *The Hiding Place*, was made into a movie by Billy Graham with World Wide Pictures in 1975.

Charles Thomas "C. T." Studd (1860–1931) from England was a pioneer missionary to China, India, and Africa. He was one of the Cambridge Seven planning to join Hudson Taylor in China.

William Carey (1761–1834) was a Baptist missionary from England. He first brought up the idea of foreign missions with a missionary manifesto called *An Enquiry into the Obligations of Christians to Use Means for the Conversion of the Heathens*. It was not easily received, but he became the "Father of Modern Missions." He is the author of the Carey Bible in Bangla, written during his time in Serampore, India.

Philip James "Jim" Elliot (1927–1956) was a missionary in Ecuador after graduating from Wheaton College. His death, at the hands of the tribal group he went to share the gospel with, was made public by a *Life* magazine article. His story, *Through Gates of Splendor*, was written by his wife, Elisabeth Elliot. More of the continuing story was chronicled in the 2006 movie, *End of the Spear*.

Viggo "Vic" Olsen (1926–present) is the medical doctor from the missionary book *Daktar: Diplomat in Bangladesh*. He worked most of his medical career as a surgeon at Memorial Christian Hospital in Bangladesh.

James "Hudson" Taylor (1832–1905) was a pioneer missionary and founder of China Inland Mission (now OMF International). He was known for his sensitivity to Chinese culture and changed the process of missions in his time. Taylor has been referred to as one of the most significant Europeans to visit China in the nineteenth century—and certainly one of the most influential missionaries, spending fifty-one years in China. He was able to preach in several Chinese dialects and is connected to the start of more than 300 stations of work and 125 schools in China.

Andrew "Brother Andrew" van der Bijl (1928–present) is a famous missionary who has earned the name "God's Smuggler," and his biography is a book of the same title. He smuggled Bibles behind the Iron Curtain into communist nations during the Cold War and the Bamboo Curtain too. Later, he brought forbidden Bibles into Islamic countries.

Robert "Bob" Pierce (1914–1978) was the founder of World Vision as well as Samaritan's Purse. He had his start working in Youth for Christ and became one of the driving forces in modern missions. Seeing hunger and suffering around the world, he penned in his Bible flyleaf, "Let my heart be broken with the things that break the heart of God."

Eric Liddell (1902–1945) was an influential Scottish athlete and famous missionary. His life is depicted in the 1981 Oscar-winning film *Chariots of Fire*. He was born in China to missionary parents and returned for service himself. He died young in a Japanese Internment Camp.

Gladys Aylward (1902–1970) was a British evangelical missionary to China. She was a pioneer against the odds herself. Her story, *Gladys Aylward: The Little Woman,* was made into a movie with Ingrid Bergman in 1958, *The Inn of the Sixth Happiness.* She was not accepted by China Inland Mission. Working as an independent missionary, she became a revered local figure. She took in children and is famous for leading over one hundred orphans over the mountains to safety against the invading Japanese. There is a Gladys Aylward Orphanage in Taiwan still.

Ralph Winter (1924–2009) was an American missiologist and Presbyterian missionary. He helped create the field of missiology itself. He founded the US Center for World Missions, William Carey International University, and the International Society for Frontier Missiology. He changed the focus and direction of the missionary movement and was named by *Time* magazine as one of the "25 Most Influential Evangelicals in America." Billy Graham stated that Ralph Winter "accelerated world evangelism." He launched the *Perspectives on World Missions* course, which is the definitive text today in missions training.

William Borden (1887–1913) was a pioneer missionary to China. He became a Christian under R. A. Torrey and went to Princeton to study ministry. As heir to the Borden fortune, he gave up everything to serve as one of the early missionaries to Muslims. He died of meningitis while serving in Egypt at only twenty-five years old. Samuel Zwemer, known as the Apostle to Islam, conducted his funeral.

G. D. Watson (1845–1924) was a Methodist minister. His poem "Others May, You Cannot," written about faithful Christian service, was found in the back of the Bible of Hudson Taylor after his death.

Recommended Readings

Aylward, Gladys, and Christine Hunter. *Gladys Aylward: The Little Woman.* Chicago: Moody Bible Institute, 1970.

Elliot, Elisabeth. *A Chance to Die: The Life and Legacy of Amy Carmichael.* New York: Fleming H. Revell Company, 1987.

Elliot, Elisabeth. *Through Gates of Splendor.* Wheaton, Ill.: Tyndale House Publishers, 1956.

Mangalwadi, Vishal, and Ruth Mangalwadi. *The Legacy of William Carey.* Wheaton, Ill.: Crossway Books, 1999.

Olsen, Viggo. *Daktar: Diplomat in Bangladesh.* Chicago: Moody Bible Institute, 1973.

St. John, Patricia. *Patricia St. John Tells Her Own Story.* Shoals, Ind.: Kingsley Press, 1993.

Taylor, Howard. *Hudson Taylor's Spiritual Secret.* Chicago: Moody Bible Institute, 1989.

Ten Boom, Corrie. *The Hiding Place.* Grand Rapids, Mich.: Chosen Books, 1971.

Winter, Ralph, ed. *Perspectives on the World Christian Movement: A Reader.* Pasadena, Calif.: William Carey Publishing, 1981.

An Opportunity to Be a Friend of Bangladesh

The Widow's Friend/ Friends of Bangladesh/ USA would be grateful for your consideration of this ministry. Through gifts from those whom God has laid on the hearts to help this work, we are able to support seven projects. There is a center for destitute women, two clinics, a school for the deaf, a hostel for young women, a children's home, and a high school. We would be grateful for your prayers and gifts.

The children of the book are mostly grown now and are learning to fold themselves in as Christians in their native land. As they have moved on, there has been no lack of needy young Bangladeshi children who fill the spots they vacated at the orphanage. In the meantime, life as a Christian in Bangladesh has not much improved. They all face many challenges, spiritually and emotionally, as they continue to mature.

The story did not at all end for the people of Bangladesh when I left. I continue to ache for them but have been unable to be there and pour my life into them anymore. There is still a great need for the widows and orphans to be supported monthly. The beautiful nakshi kanta embroidery pieces are available for purchase in the United States. The income their sales generates meets the needs of hundreds of devastatingly poor people. The work continues to grow, and the needs never let up. If God has placed the Bengalis on your heart at all—as He has mine—there are ways that you, too, can be involved in the ministry.

Jishu tomake asheerbat koro (God bless you). *Dhunnobad* (Thank you) for every prayer and every gift on behalf of the people God loves so much in Bangladesh.

The Widow's Friend   phone: 508-477-1707
PO Box 103   email: faithwillard@gmail.com
Forestdale, MA 02644

About the Author

Jill Flatt lives in Spokane, Washington, with her husband and two children. After twenty-five years of nursing, in six states and five countries, she does cardiac research now at Sacred Heart Medical Center. She still speaks Bangla to God and is in contact with many children from Home of Joy, encouraging them in their walk with the Lord.

Notes

[1] Expect Great Things: Mission quotes the inform and inspire. Compiled by Marvin J. Newell. William Carey Library 2013. Page 224.

[2] Ibid page 204.

[3] Olsen, Viggo. *Daktar: Diplomat in Bangladesh*. Chicago: Moody Bible Institute, 1973. Page 346. Used by permission.

[4] Expect Great Things: Mission quotes the inform and inspire. Compiled by Marvin J. Newell. William Carey Library 2013. Page 125.

[5] Ibid. page 55.

[6] Ibid. page 192.

[7] www.wholesomewords.org/missions/biostudd.html

[8] Expect Great Things: Mission quotes the inform and inspire. Compiled by Marvin J. Newell. William Carey Library 2013. Page 265.

[9] Missionsbox app. August 15 quote. (2013)

[10] Praise You In This Storm. Written by: John Mark Hall and Bernie Herms. 2005 Sony/ ATV Music Publishing LLC, My Refuge Music, and Publishers unknown. All right on behalf of Sony/ATV Music Publishing LLC administered by Sony/ ATV Music Publishing LLC, 8 Music Square West, Nashville, TN 37203. All rights reserved. Used by permission. Praise You In This Storm. Written by: John Mark Hall and Bernie Herms. 2005. Publishing administered by Capital CMG Publishing. PO Box 5085 Brentwood, TN 37027. All rights reserved. Used by permission.

[11] *Hold Me Jesus*. By Rich Mullins. 1996. Reunion Records.

[12] www.christianquote.com/newquote

[13] Kent, Carol. *A New Kind of Normal*. Nashville: Thomas Nelson Publishing, 2007. Used by permission.

[14] Watson, G.D. Others May, You Cannot. Public domain.

All photos used by permission.
Wedding photograph by Sarah Jane Byrnes.
Family photograph by Michael Schollenberger.